English Teacher's
SURVIVAL GUIDE

Ready-to-Use
Techniques & Materials
for Grades 7-12

MARY LOU BRANDVIK

**THE CENTER FOR APPLIED
RESEARCH IN EDUCATION**
West Nyack, New York 10995

Library of Congress Cataloging-in-Publication Data

Brandvik, Mary Lou.
    English teacher's survival guide : ready-to-use techniques and
materials for grades 7–12 / Mary Lou Brandvik.
       p.   cm.
    Includes bibliographical references.
    ISBN 0-87628-298-2
    1. Language arts (Secondary)—United States—Handbooks, manuals,
etc. 2. High school teaching—United States—Handbooks, manuals,
etc. 3. Classroom management—United States—Handbooks, manuals,
etc. 4. English teachers—United States—Handbooks, manuals, etc.
I. Title.
LB1631.B762   1994   93-43186
428′.0071′2—dc20   CIP

Printed in the United States of America

10   9   8   7   6   5   4

ISBN 0-87628-298-2

**THE CENTER FOR APPLIED RESEARCH
IN EDUCATION**

West Nyack, NY 10994

On the World Wide Web at http://www.phdirect.com

Dedication

To Sue, Diane, Joan, and the many outstanding teachers at Bemidji High School who care about their students, love teaching, and work together each day to achieve the goal of an excellent school.

Acknowledgment

Thank you to Sandra Hutchison who believed this book could and should be written and who began the editing process and to Connie Kallback whose insight and thoughtful editorial comment gave me both perspective and encouragement.

About the Author

Mary Lou Brandvik was born in Reeder, North Dakota, and spent her early school years in Hollywood, California, before returning to North Dakota. She graduated *summa cum laude* from Concordia College in Moorhead, Minnesota, with a BA in English and Art. She attended the University of Wisconsin and earned a Master's degree in English Education from the University of Illinois. She has taught in public schools in Illinois and Minnesota as well as at Bemidji State University. She has led in-service workshops in Minnesota and was a participant in the Northern Minnesota Writing Project. Ms. Brandvik chaired the Bemidji Public Schools' Writing Curriculum Committee and was selected Teacher of the Year in the Bemidji Public Schools in 1988.

In 1991 she received the Lila B. Wallace Teacher-Scholar Award from the National Endowment for the Humanities. During the sabbatical that accompanied the award, she researched the literature of the Ojibwe. She is also the author of *Writing Process Activities Kit: 75 Ready-to-Use Lessons and Worksheets for Grades 7–12.*

About This Resource

This resource will explore successful approaches to teaching English and classroom management. It is a book intended both for the new teacher who is looking for solutions to potential problems and for the more experienced teacher who may be staggering under an enormous teaching load and conflicting demands.

Most of us have chosen to be teachers of English because we love to read or write—or both—and we want to instill and nurture this same passion in our students. We want to be inspiring and provocative, caring and nurturing—a composite of the best teachers who have taught us. While thoroughly satisfying, the teaching of English is also extraordinarily demanding. The reality of the school day—interruptions, forms to fill out, bell schedules, alphabet grades, tardy slips, admits, PA announcements— drains any teacher's energy, vitality, and creativity. This book will encourage you to look at yourself and your job with a bit of selfishness. To regain or maintain the idealism that caused us to become teachers, we all need to manage and organize our professional lives in such a way that we also have time for ourselves, our families, and our lives outside the classroom.

The Survival Guide will help you do just that. It offers suggestions for beginning the year and managing and planning your classroom efficiently. It will help you organize your teaching units and design your daily lessons. It offers ideas for developing a grading philosophy and will show you ways to involve both parents and students in the evaluation process. It will help you handle controversial issues such as confidentiality and censorship and will provide numerous reproducible materials for teaching writing, reading, listening, and speaking.

All of us have heard the term "excellent school." We are told that in an excellent school, students should be doing authentic work rather than sitting in rows and working on worksheets or activities with little relevance. We are told that subjects should be integrated in order to promote intense, interesting learning activities that are meaningful to students. Instead of filling out workbook exercises to learn the mechanics of language, students should be using writing for a real readership. We are told that schools should promote and encourage collaborative activities as well as competitive ones. And, we are told, excellent schools go far beyond the standardized test routine in the evaluation of students by setting up portfolios, collections that show the progress of student work over time. Most of all, we are told, excellent schools engender an excitement and enthusiasm for learning shared by students, teachers, and parents alike.

An excellent school is everyone's goal. We each want our classroom to resemble this model as closely as possible. But how do we make it happen? Times have changed, we've changed, and our students have changed. Yesterday's lesson plans aren't meeting our needs or those of our students. Along with plenty of suggestions for writing and reading activities, the *Survival Guide* includes specific suggestions for integrating the teaching of speaking, listening, writing, and literature. It will show you how to introduce cooperative learning activities in your classroom and offer suggestions for portfolio assessment. It is intended to help you create an excellent classroom that reflects the excitement for learning that every one of us desires.

The *Survival Guide* is intended to help you handle the demands and routines of the classroom, your school system, and an evolving English curriculum so that you can face each day enthusiastically. The ideas contained in the following chapters have worked in real classrooms. They will work for you.

Mary Lou Brandvik

Table of Contents

CHAPTER I

Beginning the School Year

- *Designing a Lesson for Day One*
- *Learning Still More About Your Students*
- *Helping Students to Know One Another*

Beginning the School Year

I'll never forget my first day of teaching. I was so inexperienced that I just passed around a blank sheet of paper to take roll. I used that list to call on students for the remainder of the period. I wondered why everyone giggled when I called on George Washington and Thomas Jefferson.

It's the first day of school in your district, and it's a day fraught with capital letters for both you and your students. For the student there is The Outfit, The Supplies, The Bus Route, The Locker Assignment, The Lunch Schedule, The Teachers, The Program Schedule, The Seat Assignments. For teachers there are The Class Lists, The Bell Schedules, The Read-on-the-First-Day Announcements from the Principal's Office, The Add-or-Drop Lists of Student Names from the Counseling Office, The Student Handbook, The Fire-Drill Explanation, The Sign-up Sheet for Audiovisual Materials, The Computer Lab Schedule, and The Library Orientation Schedule. For teachers and students alike, the first day of school is, indeed, momentous: This is the day students size us up as competent or incompetent, nice or mean, fair or unfair, caring or uncaring.

One of the most important plans we make is the lesson design for the first day of the year. Some teachers spend the entire first class period making seat assignments, handing out books, and reading long lists of classroom and school regulations. If every teacher does this, and many school administrations encourage teachers to do so, a single student may hear a nearly identical set of of regulations six or seven times on the first day alone. It is not the tone most schools or classroom teachers wish to set, but it is a tone students perceive and one that's difficult to undo.

Of course, we teachers are all concerned with discipline. "Be strict in the beginning," they tell us in methods classes and in the teachers' lounge. But what happens when you let up and the students are so intimidated they are afraid to talk? There are guidelines and limits, of course. Your position tells the students you are the teacher in the classroom. How you function will tell them whether you are up to the task, and you will function best if your planning is thorough and organized. Begin setting a classroom tone and atmosphere that is right for you from the very first day of school. If you are required to read school regulations and policies, do it on a subsequent day.

DESIGNING A LESSON FOR DAY ONE

In setting the tone for your classroom, consider the following plan for the first day:

1. Welcome your students to the school and your classroom.

Take note of what is special for students on this day. If, for example, your students are ninth or tenth graders, this may be their first day in high school. They may have come from several junior highs or middle schools or from other communities. They must form new friendships and solve new problems in the more complex, less sheltered world of the high school. If they are seniors, this is the first day of their last year of high school—a time they've looked forward to with anticipation. There may be transfer students who are unfamiliar with the building or buildings and know few of their classmates. Some students are raring to get busy; others may not want to be in school at all. View your school and classroom through your students' eyes and acknowledge and honor the emotions and questions they may have concerning the new school year and your class.

2. Introduce yourself.

Give information about your own background, jobs you have held, your family, your interests. Explain why you chose teaching English as a career. Show that you are proud to be a teacher and that you value and respect your work.

3. Introduce your subject.

Be positive about the class you are teaching. Explain its benefits and elaborate on these clearly and specifically. What is it the students can expect to learn from you? What new skills will they practice and acquire? What books or novels can they look forward to reading? What units or projects do you have planned? What can they look forward to with eagerness? Be enthusiastic and inclusive as you do so. Don't expect students to "understand" why they should take a particular class. Many are enrolled only because it's required. Remember, not every student likes English and not every student hates English. However, each needs to know what he or she will learn in your classroom.

Don't qualify your first-day message by suggesting that some students will succeed while others will fail. Be sure your students understand each is beginning a new year with a clean slate. Let your students know they have a responsibility to attend class regularly, to attempt each assignment, and to participate in the class. Assure them that if each approaches the class in this manner, each can be a successful student.

4. Teach a lesson on the first day.

The first day of school, when motivation is high, is the time to make a good first impression for both students and teachers. Capitalize on this readiness by avoiding a deadly review and begin with a real lesson that will show off what both you and your students can do. Your goal on this day should be to have your students do something successfully or to learn something each can use immediately. The following exercises are a variety of nonthreatening first-day options to foster student success, help set a tone of cooperation and a sense of community in your classroom, and encourage and foster immediate student participation:

A. Have your students write answers to the following directions. Then have them use their answers as a guide while introducing themselves orally to the whole class.

1. Write your name.
2. Write the name of the city where you were born.
3. Write the name of your best subject.
4. Write the name of a difficult subject.
5. Do you have a job? If so, where? Please describe it briefly. What are some good parts of the job? Some drawbacks?
6. List three things you can do well.
7. Tell one thing your best friend doesn't know about you.

It's also possible to carry this exercise further. For example, after each person offers his or her sketch, ask the next person to speak to summarize some of what the previous student revealed. When the introductions are complete, call on individuals to identify someone in the class and to give one or two details about him or her from memory. By the end of an exercise such as this, your students will no longer be strangers to one another, and you are likely to know each student by name and also by what they are willing to reveal about themselves.

B. Pair students (preferably stranger to stranger to encourage new friendships) and ask them to spend approximately five minutes each interviewing one another. Point out that unusual questions elicit the most interesting information (for example, "What did you learn this summer that you'll remember for the rest of your life?"). Encourage students to take notes during the interview. Give them time to write a brief profile emphasizing the two most interesting things they learned about their partner. Allow students to check their information with their partners. Finally, ask each student to read the profile to the entire class. (If students seem particularly insecure about speaking and reading in front of the whole class, you might have them form groups of six to eight students to make their introductions.)

A more challenging option is to ask students to recast their profiles into another format such as a poem, lyric, letter, or story. One format that is accessible to all students is the recipe. Brainstorm with the class for a list of cooking terms such as *bake, broil, mix, whip,* and *simmer.* After you have listed several terms on the blackboard, suggest they write a recipe for the person they interviewed. The following is a sample:

Mike Peter Surprise Delight

To create this exotic senior combine:
    1 family of 8 children.
    Sift out the third youngest son.
    Beat rapidly, adding:
        clear, blue eyes,
        1 pinch of shyness,
        a heaping love of drums and carpentry.
Bake at 350° for 17 years and frost with an application
to vocational school. Serve immediately. Your guests
will be sure to ask for more.

C. Another approach to interviewing is to have the whole class interview you on the first day and move on to interviewing one another on the next day. On Day One bring to class several meaningful personal objects (mementos, documents, and a piece of clothing, for example) and encourage your students to base their questions on these. (What is it? How was it acquired? Why is it important to you? What plans do you have for its future?) Following the questioning, ask the students to write a brief profile of you either individually or collaboratively in groups to read aloud. Near the end of the period, call on students to identify those questions which produced the most information. Questions that pursue a point, for example, garner the most information.

On the following day, students bring to class three items important to each of them. Stress sentimental value as opposed to material value and the importance of keeping the items stored safely when they are not in use. Students present and explain their items to the class, and class members ask follow-up questions. Additional activities might include student-authored profiles of class members or papers based on the significance of one of the author's possessions. Final polished versions may be displayed on a bulletin board or bound as a class book for everyone to enjoy.[1]

D. Introduce the concept of freewriting or rush writing (writing without stopping or editing for a specific number of minutes). Give your students a topic such as "The quality I like best about myself is . . ." or "The best class I've ever taken was . . ." Have students write for approximately five minutes. Be sure they understand they will eventually read their writing to the class. Give them a minute or two to edit briefly and then ask each to read aloud. Some teachers let students read these early writings while seated at their desks to keep the activity nonthreatening.

If someone declines to read, suggest that you will come back to him or her after others have had a chance to read, and do so. Don't let this exercise become a showdown between you and a reluctant student. When he or she sees that other students are reading their writings aloud, this student will soon contribute, too. After everyone has read, ask the class to recall specific answers they particularly liked and to explain to the author why they liked the answer. This is an excellent way to give students positive, supportive peer feedback.

E. Students brainstorm a list of four or five chores they dislike, then select one item and write a creative excuse directed to a parent, teacher, or some other adult explaining why he or she should no longer be expected to do it. Encourage students to be as wildly imaginative as possible and discourage responses such as "I don't have my English paper today, because I had to work late at my part-time job." You may want to read the following sample aloud:

---

1. Washing the dishes
2. Cleaning the bathroom
3. Cleaning the fireplace
4. Cleaning up after the cat
5. Taking care of my younger sister.
6. ?

Mom,

I have a cut on my hand. No, it's not bleeding, but it really hurts. I know it doesn't show, but it throbs and aches. It think it could probably get infected if I stick it into greasy dishwater. And, if that happens, I might even end up in the emergency room. Then I won't be able to help you with the dishes for a long time. So <u>you</u> do them tonight, OK? I'll do them when my hand gets better—really. Just let me rest here and watch TV. Please. It doesn't throb so much in this position.

Eric

See also Chapter IV for many additional suggestions for first-day activities which involve students in collaborative work.

By introducing a first-day lesson such as one of these, you will have achieved a number of objectives: your students will have written and shared their writing with a real audience; you will have begun to establish a positive, cooperative atmosphere; you will have eliminated some of the tension and fear associated with new experiences; and, ideally, you will have shared laughter.

LEARNING STILL MORE ABOUT YOUR STUDENTS

In middle schools, junior highschools, and high schools we frequently meet 150 students a day even though the schedule breaks them into segments of twenty five to thirty five. In addition, we are expected to teach students with diverse ability levels and from varied linguistic backgrounds. To be effective at the secondary level, we need to know our students well and to get to know them as quickly as possible.

Name Tags or Student Name Plates

To take roll and learn student names, teachers have frequently begun the first day of class with assigned seating for students, and this arrangement frequently remains the same throughout the year. However, if you want your classroom seating plan to be more flexible, if you are also concerned that students learn one another's names, and if you want to begin moving students from large groups to small groups early in the year, consider distributing name tags or having each student design one of his or her own.

Another option is to have students fold a large sheet of notebook paper into thirds and to have them print their names in large letters on the middle section of the folded paper. The paper will sit upright on a desk, and the teacher and the students are able to read one another's names easily. (See Figure A.) Students may keep these name sheets in their notebooks and begin the first few weeks of classes by placing this identification on their desks. This is also a useful and helpful way to identify students when guest speakers are invited into the classroom.

FIGURE A

Questionnaires

Some information about your students will be available prior to the first day of school in cumulative records, tests results, and in discussions with other teachers (but don't let negative comments color your perspective). You may be able to receive information about a student's health status from the school nurse, but you may have to seek it out. It will also be possible to ask for additional information about students during parent-teacher conferences. However, much of this information will come to you later in the school year. Consequently, you may wish to design and distribute student questionnaires or inventories at the beginning of the year and at other appropriate times throughout the school year. Questionnaires such as 1.1 "Getting Acquainted", 1.2 "Getting to Know You," 1.3 "Reading Inventory," and 1.4 "Writing Inventory" (which you may duplicate in their entirety or use as a basis for developing your own) are useful in surveying student interests, experiences, spoken languages, favorite subjects, friends, classroom expectations, and ability to study at home. This information will help you know your students more quickly and will be an immediate aid in planning your curriculum and in designing both large- and small-group activities.

Name _____ Date _____

1.1 Getting Acquainted

Some of my friends call me by my nickname, _____.

Right now, I'm _____ years old, and my birthday is _____.

I live with (names, and relation to you) _____

_____

_____ at the following address:

_____.

My phone number is _____.

My best subject in school is _____, and my

most difficult subject is _____.

My favorite kind of music is _____ and

my favorite song is _____.

My favorite after-school activity is _____.

One thing that makes me happy is _____

_____

_____,

and I am really sad when _____

_____

_____.

Someday, I hope to _____

_____

_____

_____

_____

_____

_____.

1.2 Getting to Know You

1. Suppose you are a major character in one of your favorite

   books. What is your name? _____

2. In what book do you appear?_____

3. Write the names of five people you don't know but would like to.

   _____

   _____

   _____

   _____

   _____

4. Name five things you can do as well as or better than anyone else.

   _____

   _____

   _____

   _____

   _____

5. Many authors have used pen names to substitute for their own.

   Invent a pen name for yourself: _____

   Explain your choice below.

   _____

   _____

   _____

   _____

   _____

   _____

Name _____ Date _____

1.3 Reading Inventory

Reading is one of the most valuable things we do. As we work to develop our skills, it is helpful to understand how our attitudes have been formed. Please answer the following questions about your own reading history.

1. When you were a young child did your parents or someone else read

   to you or tell you bedtime stories? _____ If so, what were your favorites?

   _____

2. What fairy tales or children's rhymes can you recall by heart? _____

   _____

   _____

   _____

3. Were there books and magazines in your house? _____

   If so, who read them? _____

   Did you see your parents or other adults reading? _____

4. Did you go to a nursery school, a Head Start center, or a local library

   where stories were read aloud to you? _____

   Did you like the stories? _____

5. Did you watch TV as a child? _____ If yes, did you watch the reading segments on

   education television shows, such as *Sesame Street?* and did you enjoy them? _____

6. If yes, what other kinds of shows did you watch on television? _____

   _____

   Did you watch the commercials? _____ Are there any

   jingles that you still remember? _____ If so, recall an example.

   _____

7. Were you given books as presents or rewards? _____ If so, please explain:

_____

_____

8. What were some of your favorite childhood books? _____

_____

_____

9. Recall the names of some of the teachers who taught you to read in school.

_____

Try to remember how they taught you. Explain: _____

_____

_____

10. Did your teachers read to you? _____ At a certain grade level, did

they stop reading to you? _____ Did they ever talk about

what they read? _____

11. Did you enjoy reading in school or did you read just because it was required?

_____

_____

12. Do you recall having to read aloud in front of the class? _____

If so, how did you feel doing this? _____

_____

13. As you entered junior high school did you enjoy reading? _____

Did you begin to read more or less frequently? _____ Please

explain. _____

_____

_____

14. Did your junior high school friends read? _____ Was there peer pressure on

you to read or not read? Please explain. _____

_____

_____

15. What is the best book you've ever read? _____

What made it best? _____

_____

16. What is the worst book you have ever read? _____

Did you finish it? _____ Who or what made you read it?

_____

17. What magazines or newspapers do you look at regularly? _____

_____

_____

18. Where and when do you like to read? _____

_____

_____

19. What book are you reading at the present time? _____

_____

How did you choose it? _____

_____

20. What books are you considering reading next? _____

_____

_____

_____

_____

21. Do you have friends who enjoy reading and with whom you can talk about books?

_____

22. Do you buy books and keep them?_____ If so, where do you keep

them? _____

23. In general, how do you feel about reading? _____

_____

_____

_____

_____

1.4 Writing Inventory

1. When you are given a writing assignment, how do you approach it?

   Circle one.

   a. I look forward to it.   c. I'm sure I will fail.

   b. I don't know how to begin.   d. With a feeling I can do OK.

2. What are your major strengths as a writer?

   _____

   _____

   _____

   _____

3. What weaknesses do you have in writing?

   _____

   _____

   _____

   _____

4. Describe one of the most interesting writing assignments you've ever been asked to do. Why did you find it interesting?

   _____

   _____

   _____

   _____

5. What is the worst writing assignment you can recall having?

   _____

   _____

   _____

   _____

Writing Inventory, continued

What made it so terrible? _____

_____

_____

_____

6. Have you ever kept a journal? _____ Do you keep a journal or diary now? _____ If so, explain how you began and what it means to you.

_____

_____

_____

_____

_____

7. How do you define good writing?

_____

_____

_____

_____

_____

_____

_____

_____

_____

_____

_____

_____

_____

_____

HELPING STUDENTS TO KNOW ONE ANOTHER

We often make the assumption that most students in our classes know one another. They may not, and if they do, it is likely to be a superficial acquaintance. A shy student may sit for months alongside students whose names he or she doesn't know. Short get-acquainted activities at the beginning of a class period are well worth the class time, especially if you wish to promote a feeling of cooperation and trust within the group.

Opening Exercises

Occasionally, as part of the opening exercise, encourage students to move around the room talking with one another and finding the answers to one or two questions that you've written on the blackboard. For example:

- Who in this class drives the oldest car?
- Who walked to school this morning?
- Who skipped breakfast this morning?
- Whose first language is not English?
- Who has a part-time job he or she really enjoys?
- Who has an unusual job or once had one?
- Who has an exotic pet?
- Who has an unusual hobby?
- Which student in this class gets up the earliest in the morning?
- Which student in this class works the latest hours at night?

A Whole-Class Get-Acquainted Activity

A series of sequenced questions which encourage students to take risks, to respond honestly, and to get positive reinforcement for doing so is helpful for setting a positive class climate. The following activity requires a full class period.

1. Seat the group in a large circle. The group leader or the teacher participates as well and answers first. Note: Some students may elect to "pass" temporarily on any question. Come back to them when all others have answered.
2. Ask each person to give his or her first name. The students take turns repeating the names of every person in the circle.
3. Ask each person in turn, "If you were a musical instrument, what instrument would you be and why?"
4. Ask each person, "If you were an animal, what animal would you be and why?"
5. Ask each person, "What is one thing of which you are proud?"
6. Ask each person in the group to choose one other person's response to the preceding question and to tell that person why he or she especially likes that response. Make sure members address each other directly by name: "Tony, I liked your answer because . . ." Don't allow a response such as, "I liked Tony's response because . . ."

7. If time is limited, stop here. You'll want students to respond in writing to this exercise. It's good to end on a positive note. If there is plenty of time, continue on.

8. Ask each person, "If you could change one thing about yourself, what would you change and why?"

9. Repeat activity 6 in response to question 8.

10. Ask students to respond in writing to this activity. How did they feel about doing it? What did they like? Dislike? What did they learn? Collect the papers and, without correcting, read them to learn more about your students and their reactions to this type of activity.

CHAPTER II

Managing Your Classroom

- *Arranging the Room*
- *Planning for Books, Paper, and Equipment*
- *Planning an Efficient Classroom*
- *Devising a Fair Grading System*

CHAPTER II

Managing Your Classroom

Please, Richard, leave that window closed. I know it's 98 degrees in here, but with the noise outside from the lawn mower and garbage truck, I can't hear Heather's question.

Effective teachers organize their space, materials, auxiliary personnel, and students to create a pleasant and effective environment for learning.

ARRANGING THE ROOM

Spend time planning the layout of desks and materials before students arrive in the fall. Maybe you're one of those lucky teachers with a state-of-the-art classroom—the kind with plenty of storage space, bulletin boards and chalkboards, lots of electronic gadgets, and, best of all, plenty of extra space for specialized learning and activity centers. It's more probable, though, that your classroom is cramped, dingy, and poorly ventilated. You may have gotten into the habit of arranging student desks in rows all year long because nothing else seems possible or as efficient. But, even the most unlikely room presents some options, and you should try for a variation from time to time. Figures B, C, D, and E illustrate some options.

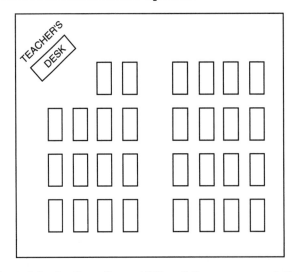

Figure B—Students' desks face the middle of the room, and the focus is away from the teacher. This is an ideal configuration when students are reading aloud.

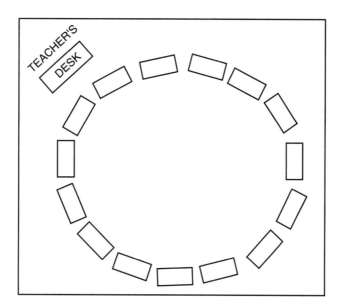

Figure C—Desks are arranged in a large circle. This enables each student to see every other student in the classroom. The teacher becomes a member of the circle and his or her position as the one authority figure is de-emphasized. This arrangement is ideal for class discussion and is less threatening for shy students who fear speaking at the front of the room.

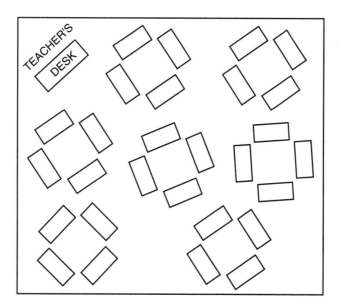

Figure D—Desks are arranged in twos, threes, or fours for small-group work. Group members face one another and are close enough to communicate effectively. It's best to have plenty of space in order to separate groups, which naturally tend to become louder as everyone actively participates. You will want to have a clear access lane to each group. If classroom space is limited, consider moving one or two groups to the hall or to an empty neighboring classroom for small-group activities. If students work in groups in the hall, ask that they move their desks or chairs and a table there as well. Sitting on the floor isn't conducive to serious group work.

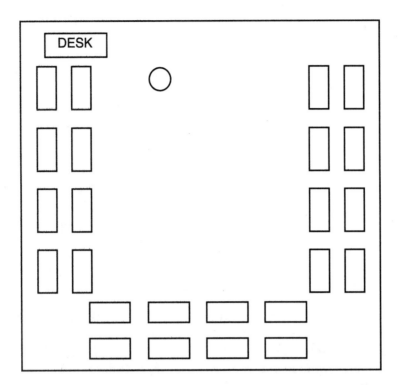

Figure E—Desks are arranged in a horseshoe, with the teacher's chair or stool at the open end. This arrangement allows students to see one another, and the teacher is able to move easily from student to student whenever necessary. Some teachers who wish to emphasize the cooperative nature of their classrooms eliminate a lectern or designated spot from which to speak and turn their desks to a wall to eliminate the suggestion of a barrier between students and themselves.

An option you might consider for combating monotony is to move your class to other settings in or near the school from time to time. Is there a lawn, a park, a playground, or an art gallery nearby where your class might write or read poetry or give presentations? Why not occasionally move to a small auditorium, the library, or an empty classroom, or exchange classrooms with another teacher for a period? Students need variety in their lives, and so do teachers.

PLANNING FOR BOOKS, PAPER, AND EQUIPMENT

Students should know where reading and writing materials are kept in the classroom and what is available for their use.

1. Designate a specific location for equipment and materials such as the following:

- pens, pencils, and colored markers
- lined and unlined paper in a variety of sizes and colors
- construction paper
- poster board
- stationery and envelopes

- staplers, staples, and staple removers
- tape
- gluesticks, glue, or paste
- scissors
- paper clips
- erasers and correction fluid
- index cards
- rubber bands
- paper punch
- transparent tape
- rubber cement
- tape recorder and blank tapes
- overhead projector, transparencies, and markers
- typewriter or word processor and printer
- television and VCR

It's good to have all of these materials available in the classroom. Students should be encouraged, however, to have their own paper, pens, and pencils. They should also know where they might find them in the classroom on an emergency basis. Pencils and pens tend to disappear quickly, and some teachers tell their students, "These materials are here for you to use, but once they're gone, I won't replace them. Be thoughtful of others."

2. Decide where reference materials such as dictionaries, thesauruses, and usage handbooks are to be kept. If you expect to allow students to use these materials outside the classroom, plan a clear checkout procedure.

Ideally, your classroom should be equipped with a dictionary (containing etymologies) and a thesaurus for every student. It may be possible to store these on or below each student's desk. However, the books tend to disappear from the room as students gather them with their own books. Keep resource books in easily accessible bookcases and require students to consult them frequently. Students who do not have access to these materials at home should be encouraged to check them out on a form such as form 2.1, "Sign-Out Sheet," which is displayed in a prominent place.

2.1 Sign-Out Sheet Teacher _____ Room _____

Student's Name (Please print)	Hour	Material Checked Out (include book title and number)	Date Out	Date In

It's helpful to have an atlas and an almanac nearby, as well as colorful, laminated maps of the United States and the world. Other books you might want to have available are:

- atlas of historical fiction or fantasy,
- rhyming dictionary,
- *Reader's Companion to World Literature*,
- *Guiness Book of World Records*,
- *Dictionary of Classical Mythology*,
- collection of single titles of novels, poetry, and short stories
- magazines such as *The Writer, Voice, Literary Cavalcade, Sassy*, and *Merlyn's Pen*.

Booklets of writings by previous students should also be available. Photographs of art works, diagrams of theaters and other sites, videos about authors or settings, recordings of literature, and tapes of music contemporary with literary works are all excellent additions to any language arts classroom.

PLANNING AN EFFICIENT CLASSROOM

Be clear about your expectations and management style. Give students as many responsibilities as possible. Enable them to go about their business of being independent, productive students without interrupting you with unnecessary, time-consuming questions such as "May I borrow a pencil?" The goal is to create a self-starting classroom, a classroom filled with students who come into class and begin work immediately.

Students should know what to bring to class each day.

It is desirable for every student to have a copy of whatever material is being studied. Students should be expected to bring the appropriate material to class each day. Hand out short-term or unit schedules (see Chapter 3), and make your expectations specific and clear.

Have a clear plan for obtaining forgotten materials.

If practical, allow students to leave the classroom to retrieve forgotten materials. Encourage them to do so as quickly and with as little commotion as possible. One effective means of discouraging this practice is to be sure students who have to leave the classroom to gather forgotten materials understand they will be given an unexcused tardy for the class period.

Explain the procedure for leaving your classroom.

Do all in your power to discourage the tendency for heavy traffic in and out of your classroom—to the library, the office, or the lavatory, for example. Many teachers tell students they may leave the classroom only at the end of the class period if all other work is completed or when there is an obvious, valid emergency. Many schools expect teachers to issue hall passes for situations like this. To avoid writing passes for each occasion, some teachers make out and laminate a master pass. Others resort to a block of wood with the word *pass* and the teacher's name and room number on it. The point of the block of wood is that it's too large and cumbersome for students to lose or to inadvertently leave in a pocket. It should be assigned a specific location in the classroom.

Plan for distributing and collecting materials.

Consider using *one* of the following time-saving suggestions for distributing or collecting materials.

- If possible, put materials on students' desks before class begins.
- Designate a few students to distribute materials and to collect assignments and place them in a specified location.
- Place a table or desk near the classroom door, and lay out materials for students to collect as they enter the classroom.
- Set up a file folder for each student. When students enter the classroom, they quickly check their folders for the day's materials. This method can also save time in distributing makeup materials to absent students. If you are a teacher who must "float" from room to room, make arrangements with the teacher whose room you are using for a bit of space of your own—a shelf on a bookcase and a drawer in a file cabinet, for example.
- Distribute materials in packets rather than as separate handouts.

Design an efficient means of taking roll.

If you prefer to take attendance yourself, one time-saving approach is to introduce the day's activity or assignment, and after your students are involved in their work, take a minute or two to complete the attendance form. Many teachers who have their students keep either a reading or writing journal regularly set aside the first five minutes or so of each period for writing. During this time the teacher quickly takes roll and then writes along with the students.

Another approach is to appoint one or two students in each class as attendance takers. The small amount of effort and time necessary at the beginning of the year to explain the procedure will ultimately allow you to move quickly to your teaching objectives. Place a master list or master seating chart and a stack of forms, (such as form 2.2, "Absence and Tardiness Report") in a designated location and explain these to the responsible students. Each day one of these students fills in an attendance sheet. (It's unwise to give students access to your grade book.) Late students entering the classroom are instructed to present their admit passes to the attendance-taker rather than to you.

2.2   Absence and Tardiness Report

DAY _____   DATE _____   MONTH _____

CLASS _____

HOUR _____

TEACHER _____

ABSENT STUDENTS, EXCUSED (Please write clearly)

_____   _____

_____   _____

_____   _____

ABSENT STUDENTS, UNEXCUSED

_____   _____

_____   _____

_____   _____

TARDY STUDENTS, EXCUSED

_____   _____

_____   _____

_____   _____

TARDY STUDENTS, UNEXCUSED

_____   _____

_____   _____

_____   _____

ATTENDANCE-TAKER'S SIGNATURE _____

Attach all passes to this sheet and return to the classroom teacher at the end of the class period.

Organize and plan for makeup work.

Each day write a brief summary of the day's lesson, activities, and assignments on a dated index card. Place the card in a file box in a designated spot in the classroom. When absent students return, they will quickly learn the efficient habit of checking these summaries for makeup assignments. You may prefer a spiral-bound notebook, which ensures that the materials stay together and in order.

Ideally, students should take turns writing these summaries. Often we teachers do the work ourselves because it seems expedient. It's well worth your time—and it's a legitimate learning activity—if you organize a dated schedule for your students to follow as they take turns writing the summaries. The following is a sample set of directions for students who are writing daily summaries:

1. Write the date: day, month, date, and year.
2. List the names of students who are absent.
3. Write a summary of what happened in class on this day.
4. Collect handouts (if there are any) for people who are absent.
5. Write the name of an absent student on each handout.
6. Place the handouts in the appropriate file box.
7. Sign your name.

Call on the writer on the following day to read his or her summary aloud. In assuming this responsibility, students gain experience in summary writing and are immediately aware they are writing for a real audience. The summary, itself, is a good review of the previous day's work and leads smoothly into the next assignment or activity.

Whenever you hand out materials or give tests, instruct your student helpers or remember yourself to write the names of absent students on a copy of each handout. Then place this material on a shelf devoted to materials for that particular class period. Students seeking makeup work will find it easily, and you'll avoid having to rummage through stacks of old handouts or your filing cabinet. (You'll want to keep makeup tests elsewhere, however.)

Another form which can be helpful in dealing with students who have serious makeup difficulties is shown below:

Student _____

Class _____

Dates missed _____

Makeup work:

Last date to submit work: _____

Student Signature _____

Teacher Signature _____

The teacher itemizes the missed assignments on this form, provides handouts and explanations, and sets a due date for the work. Make a carbon copy or photocopy of the completed form so that both student and teacher have a copy. Both student and teacher sign the form, and the student attaches his or her copy to the makeup work when it is handed in.

To avoid having assorted papers tossed on your desk just as you are preparing to begin a class, clearly label baskets or boxes for each class period, and instruct students where to place daily assignments and makeup work.

Use student aides to perform routine tasks.

In some schools, students will seek out teachers and ask to be designated as student aides. It is also possible to enlist the help of a study hall teacher in finding students who are willing to give up a study hall period to work in a teacher's classroom. Ideally, the student will be available during your preparation time to help you in the following ways:

- run errands or deliver and collect materials;
- set up equipment such as filmstrip projectors, tape recorders, or VCRs (you may have to train a student to handle these tasks, but that student will then be able to train others);
- sort and staple materials;
- place materials in students' file folders;
- put up or take down displays of classroom work;
- water plants and keep the room neat and organized; and
- correct simple multiple choice or true and false quizzes and tests. (Some schools have electronic scanners for correcting true and false or multiple choice tests. If one is available, instruct your aide in its operation. For the sake of privacy, you may want to assign numbers to students for test taking and posting grades. Some teachers simply assign students the same number as that next to the student's name in the grade book. Record all marks yourself, however. Students should not have access to your grade book.)

Involve students in decorating the classroom.

You'll want your classroom to be attractive and comfortable. Give students some ownership in the process of creating bulletin boards and displays. Ask them to choose from your collection of posters and decide where these should be placed. Display as much student work as possible. Add plants, a comfortable old couch or chairs—even window curtains—if space permits and this reflects your personal style.

As you plan your teaching units, suggest bulletin board and display projects to students as part of their individual assignment options. Student-made bulletin boards are not new, of course, but you can be assured that projects such as these are worthwhile learning activities for the students themselves as well as timesavers for you. Displays created by students within the classroom elicit high interest and responses from their peers and offer a legitimate opportunity for students to recast their ideas in a visual manner. Ask students to donate examples of outstanding work to your own classroom collection. These samples can serve as models for subsequent classes, and students enjoy knowing you admire their work enough to save and display it. Don't, however, recycle the same materials over and over. If you're short of display space, cover a wall with colored paper for thematic or seasonal murals or string wires or fishing line from wall to wall. Then attach material to be displayed to the line with colorful clothes pins or clips. Older students enjoy the unexpected, too.

The way we each use time reflects our individual teaching priorities and teaching methods. When we enable students to become an asset to our classroom management style, we provide them with valuable responsibility and experience and we free ourselves from some of the tasks that can overwhelm our teaching efforts.

Create a positive design for discipline within the classroom.

The most effective teachers seem to have fewer problems with discipline; yet, no single description applies to them all. Some are charismatic and have great personal warmth, while others are more formal and somewhat aloof. Some exude an exuberant enthusiasm, while others are gentle and congenial. Despite such personality and style differences there seems to be a common thread that characterizes such teachers. Studies suggest that effective teachers (through everything they do) communicate "We want to be here." They believe in the value of their discipline and are committed to it. They care about the students and expect a great deal from them. In addition, their classrooms and teaching plans are so well organized and managed there is frequently little time or opportunity for discipline problems.[1]

We often hear our colleagues lament about how students have changed, how difficult it is to teach today. In many ways this is true. Family structure has changed, society has changed, and discipline can be a tough, complex job. One teacher recalls worrying about squirt guns twenty-five years ago, but today, he points out, he has metal detectors in his school. To be realistic, the majority of students we meet and teach each day are cooperative and anxious to please. A smaller number will work hard if we give them rules and plenty of structure. A very small percentage have real behavior problems and challenge discipline. They are the ones who can "drive a teacher crazy" or into retirement.[2]

Researchers suggest that the basic needs (survival, belonging, power, freedom, and fun) of our most defiant students are not being met. Many of these students are barely surviving. They may be abused, hungry, homeless, or unloved. As a classroom teacher you cannot solve all their problems, but you do need to understand what is happening at home, and you do need to involve the school's support staff. Your classroom, despite their behavior, may be the only safe place these students know. As a teacher you can provide a setting that is predictable. You can tell them the rules, state the consequences if they break the rules, and provide the structure that is lacking in their lives. These students need to feel they belong someplace, and they need to feel they have some power over their lives. Provide opportunities for choices and options for assignments. Like every other person in your class, these students need a chance to succeed, and they need honest, positive recognition when they do. Troublemakers are often students who have too little to do or who cannot do what is assigned. Shorten assignments. Try to make the goal of each assignment clearer and more immediately attainable. Monitor their progress frequently and involve them in their own self-evaluation.

In dealing with this type of student, we must also remember that we cannot control other people, only ourselves. The best classroom teacher is not the boss, but a manager who avoids power struggles and who gives students the responsibility and the opportunity to succeed.[3] Good managers have few rules, and these are specific and positive. Some teachers solicit their students' ideas and suggestions because they feel students are more likely to implement rules they have helped develop. Concerns which routinely need to be addressed include:

- tardiness
- late homework assignments
- disruptive behavior
- dismissal procedures

The following guidelines are helpful as you or you and your students design rules for your classroom:

1. Limit the number of rules. Five or six positive rules are best.
2. Design rules that encourage student learning.
3. State the rules in language students understand.
4. Determine in advance the consequences of keeping and breaking rules.
5. Print and distribute the rules to each class member.[4]

Some teachers also ask students and their parents to sign a verification form acknowledging that they have read and agreed to the list. See form 2.3, "Classroom Regulations."

2.3 Classroom Regulations   Class _____   Teacher _____

1. **REQUIRED MATERIALS.** Bring the following materials to class each day:

   A. pencil
   B. pen
   C. notebook paper
   D. English folder
   E. book for reading

2. **TARDINESS.** You are expected to be in your desk with the required materials and reading book when the bell rings. If you are not there, you will be marked tardy.

3. **CLASSROOM BEHAVIOR.** Your responsibilities in this class are:

   A. to attend class regularly;
   B. to be on time;
   C. to be prepared for class;
   D. to meet deadlines (all assignments due at the <u>beginning</u> of each class on the due date);
   E. to use your time wisely;
   F. to be actively involved as a member of a group;
   G. to have a positive attitude; and
   H. to pay attention, listen, and not be disruptive.

   All students are expected to be positive, contributing members in this class. Be polite and thoughtful of one another. If your behavior prevents our class from functioning well, I will talk with you privately. No one will ever be publicly embarrassed or threatened. If unacceptable behavior continues, I will ask to meet with you and one of the principals. If this meeting is not helpful, I will ask to meet with you, a principal, and a parent or guardian.

4. **ABSENCES AND MAKEUP WORK.** You are expected to make up any work missed because of any absence. Check the card file for a summary of the work you have missed. If anything is unclear, see me about a further explanation. You will be given two days to make up major assignments. After that time, points will be deducted for lateness. However, it will be nearly impossible for you to make up many in-class group activities if you are absent. In some cases, I will give you alternative assignments, and you will need to confer with me about options. If you know beforehand that you will be absent, please inform me so that I can help you plan your makeup work. The quality of your work will be higher if you attend class regularly and meet all deadlines.

5. **DISMISSAL.** I will dismiss you at the end of each class period.

6. **GRADED PAPERS AND HANDOUTS.** Keep all graded papers and handouts in your English folder for reference. At the end of each quarter, we will discard any unneeded papers:

© 1994 by The Center for Applied Research in Education

If a difficult student is causing a problem, keep a written, dated log of any classroom incidents. When a conference becomes necessary, you will have an accurate record of what has occurred. The following is a format which is a useful guideline for a conference with a student or students and parents.

1. Student's Name: Date:

2. Description of behavior:

3. What are the student's strengths, interests, and goals?

4. What is the student feeling in my class?

5. What do I need the student to do in my class?

6. What specific steps can I try?

7. What can the student do?

Despite the fact that the 1990s bring us a new generation of students who present increasing challenges, we can still do many things successful teachers have been doing for a long time. We can be prepared for class, care about our students, and have fair expectations for them. We can show our enthusiasm for English, use our class time for teaching and learning, balance our goals with the interests of our students, look for the root of behavioral problems, and use fair, positive, and prompt measures to address discipline problems. Most important, we must stay emotionally detached from tense discipline situations.

DEVISING A FAIR GRADING SYSTEM

Grades are meant to reflect the quality of each student's performance in the classroom. They are intended to be both a means of communicating with students and parents and a method of record keeping. Colleges ask about class rank. Businesses inquire about grades. What makes grading so troublesome for teachers is that an abstract symbol does not adequately express the complexities of a student's growth and says nothing about interest, involvement, cooperation, competency, improvement, or effort, for example. (Chapters 4, 5, 6, and 7 discuss in detail the evaluation and grading of writing, reading, listening, speaking, and cooperative activities.)

Grading Scales

How we handle the whole issue of grading and grades is important. As concerned teachers, we want to arrive at a fair system for computing grades, a system that best reflects the student's work in our classroom. In designing a grading system, many teachers use a grading scale like the following:

95%–100% = A	90%–100% = A
85%–94% = B	80%–89% = B
75%–84% = C	70%–79% = C
70%–74% = D	60%–69% = D
0%–69% = F	0%–59% = F

In some schools teachers choose their own scale. Others have a schoolwide or departmentwide policy which determines the scale.

Every assigned activity or exercise carries a total number of possible points. Major assignments are allotted a greater number of points than short quizzes or exercises. The actual points accumulated by the student are added, and the student's total is divided by the number of possible points to determine the student's percentage. This percentage is converted to a letter grade based on whatever scale the teacher is using and becomes the grade the student "earns" for a grading period. A variation based on such a scale can be achieved by indicating what kinds of effort will affect the final grade in a particular way. For example, you may decide that unit tests will count for 20 percent of the grade, daily grades another 30 percent, writing, 30 percent, and group projects, 20 percent. This will involve more time in computation, but the advantage is that it will give you more specific information for parent- teacher conferences. Although it gives the appearance of objectivity, this approach is also variable and subjective.

In conjunction with grading scales, many teachers who have access to computers are beginning to use computer programs for recording and reporting student grades. These programs not only make it possible for you to closely monitor each student's total points and grade percentage, but they also perform a variety of computations such as final percentages, grades, and class averages. It is possible to print a spreadsheet report for an entire class or for an individual student at any time throughout a grading period. The individual reports are especially helpful in conferences with students at mid-quarter reporting time or as a resource for parent-teacher conferences. As useful as these programs are, however, entering the data into the program takes time. A computer program should never be used to replace your grade book, which must always be kept as a backup.

Portfolio Grades

More and more teachers and schools are turning to portfolios, samples of actual school work, to help evaluate student progress. Portfolio grades are generally not used to determine a student's entire grade for a marking period. It is a single grade averaged with others earned throughout a grading period to determine a student's final grade. Those who encourage teachers to use portfolios in the classroom do so because they believe we need to look at a student's growth and development over time. In addition, they emphasize that portfolios become a partnership involving students and teachers and teachers and parents. Portfolios can be the focal point of a student-teacher conference or a parent-teacher conference. They are especially effective in fostering parent involvement because parents get a chance to see and understand their child's work instead of just looking at letter grades. Used effectively, a portfolio will help you assess your students, involve your students in their own assessment, and, most important, promote further learning in your students.

There are enormous variations, however, in the way portfolios can be used. It's important to distinguish between writing folders and portfolios. Writing folders generally contain all the writing (including drafts) a student has produced. Portfolios, on the other hand, contain representative samples of a student's efforts in several areas. In combination with reading and speaking activities, they may become hefty collections of reading logs, photographs of projects or the projects themselves, video and audio recordings of dramatic responses, as well as self-evaluations by the student, evaluations by peers, and evaluative material by the teacher.

If you plan to use portfolios, you'll want to avoid making them a collection of everything a student has done. This can become messy, hard work for you or just another file of papers you must shuffle and store. The portfolio is a collection which is assembled by the student, and it is meant to illustrate the student's efforts, progress, or achievements. The best portfolios:

- have a clear plan for selecting the material to be included;
- involve students in the selection of the pieces to be included; and
- encourage self-reflection on the part of students.[5]

Teachers have created a variety of formats for portfolios. For example, some use the portfolio exclusively for the writing portion of their courses. These teachers have their students assemble several pieces of writing along with a written rationale for why they were selected, sometimes in the form of a letter to the teacher. Portfolios, however, need not be used exclusively for writing. They may also include student samples from a variety of reading, writing, listening, and speaking activities.

Getting started with portfolios.

Portfolios are easiest to manage if you begin by handing out a file folder to each student and indicating a filing cabinet or location in the room where these are to be kept. Make a rule that the entire portfolio should never leave the classroom (only single papers) to ensure that students do not lose their work. Decide before you begin what you want students to place in their folders and turn this list into a table of contents. If you wish students to include examples of a variety of activities and assignments, consider the following sample. Remind students to carefully date and label all materials and to organize them in the order you indicate on your list.

Sample portfolio table of contents.

1. The beginning of the year writing and reading inventories.
2. A writing from early in the quarter (or grading period) with all drafts and pre-writing materials attached as well as self-evaluation materials, peer conference notes, and teacher's conference comments. (The number of writings and variety of formats will depend upon the age and ability of the particular students.)
3. A writing from later in the quarter with all additional material.
4. A self-evaluation of your journal writing.
5. A brief description of a cooperative group literature project in which you participated.
6. A self-evaluation of your contribution to the group project.
7. A self-evaluation of the group's project.
8. A self-evaluation of your work for the grading period.
9. A statement of your goals for the next grading period.
10. Your teacher's response to the portfolio. (See form 2.4, "Describe Your Work in This Class.")

Plan to assess student portfolios periodically, every four weeks or so, and include notes about your observations. Some teachers also attach a grade to these observations.

Additional Suggestions for Involving Students in the Evaluation Process

Evaluation is an ongoing process intended to help students understand their strengths and weaknesses as learners. Previously we teachers assumed the role of sole evaluator in the classroom, and we thought of evaluation as a part of our grading process. Today, we are learning to involve students because we've come to understand that self-reflection is a significant component of the learning process.

You'll want to plan for a variety of ways to encourage your students to respond to and assess their own work. Form 2.4, "Describe Your Work in This Class," is helpful for involving students in self-assessment and may be used in conjunction with a portfolio or in preparation for teacher-student or parent-teacher conferences. If saved, the form, itself, becomes a record of student growth. Ideally, you will have several of these in each student's file by the end of the year.

Name _____ Date _____

2.4   Describe Your Work in This Class

As this grading period comes to an end, I am required to assign a grade which characterizes the quality of your work. I want you to help me with this process by completing this sheet. I value your input as I make my final determination of grades.

1. (Circle One)   I   always   contribute positively to this class.
                               usually
                               sometimes
                               never

2. My assignments are   always   handed in on time.
                               usually
                               sometimes
                               never

3. I attend class regularly.
   I am absent occasionally.
   My absences are frequent.

4. My makeup work is   always   completed.
                               usually
                               seldom

5. I work to the best of my ability in this class.
   I do enough to get by.
   I do as little as possible in this class.

6. I believe the grade I deserve and have earned is_____

   because _____

   _____

   _____

   _____

   _____

   _____

   _____

   _____

   _____

One important thing I have learned this grading period is _____

_____

_____

_____

_____

_____

_____

My goals for next quarter are

_____

_____

_____

_____

_____

Student's signature _____

Teacher's response:

_____

_____

_____

_____

_____

_____

_____

Teacher's signature _____

This type of self-evaluation form will help you gain further insight into a student's understanding of himself or herself and is an excellent way in which to help students set personal goals for the next unit or grading period. Used just prior to parent-teacher conferences, it helps cut misunderstandings with parents to a minimum. It is also possible, although less desirable, to mail copies of the student-completed forms to parents or guardians who do not attend a teacher conference.

Suggestions for Your Gradebook

- Plan to record at least one grade per student each week in your grade book. Not every grade needs to reflect a major assignment. Give a variety of weekly quizzes or exercises that can be easily evaluated and graded. Without such a plan, you may arrive at the mid-quarter (when deficiency notices are due) lacking information to keep parents informed about the progress of their child. It's simply not fair to fail a student at the end of the quarter if you haven't earlier notified him or her and the parents of this possibility. On the other hand, an occasional student will receive a passing mark at mid-quarter, yet do so little work after that, that he or she is failing by the time final grades are due. If you realize this is occurring, make an effort to reach a parent or guardian by mail or telephone. With 130 to 150 students, it may not be possible for you to keep track of each student this closely, although the computer programs are especially helpful in monitoring students' points and percentages regularly. A computer printout listing the student's earned points or a folder of the student's earlier and later work is helpful supporting information for the times when such a situation occurs.

- Grade more than just written work. For example, if one student gives an oral presentation, grade the other students on their listening skills. Students might earn points by repeating or writing down one fact they have learned from the report or explaining one detail they like about the report. Devise a variety of ways to give grades, because it is within that variety that you achieve the most fairness.[6]

- Check assignments at the beginning of a class period, and be sure that students understand they will lose points if the work is not complete. If you use this approach consistently, the percentage of students who arrive in class each day with their homework done will rise significantly.

- When students are absent give them zeroes for short in-class quizzes or assignments—then average in the zeroes. At the same time, allow students to earn extra points for extra credit work, but be sure the additional work is appropriate and reinforces or expands upon what is happening in the class. Although this will take extra time on your part, it is worthwhile because it underscores the importance of good class attendance without penalizing any student unfairly. Good students who are legitimately absent once or twice find this approach fair because they are given the option of making up the points.

- The work a student does in the last few weeks of a quarter or semester should probably have a greater impact on the final grade than the work early in the course. In the case of writing, if a student's writing has improved, weighing all writing equally isn't a good idea.

- If points are averaged and sit equally between two grades, choose the higher grade if the student's work has improved over the course of the grading period. Choose the lower grade if the quality of the student's work has declined.

- If a student disagrees with the grade you've assigned for a particular test or paper, be willing to talk about it and change the grade if reasonable. Plenty of in-class conferences will help eliminate these kinds of problems as will plenty of student self-evaluation.

- Unless your school has a policy against this, collect and keep all major tests after they've been returned and explained to the students. Making out tests takes time, and if you are likely to use them again, keep them out of circulation. A student's writing, however, should be his or hers to keep. Students are pleased, however, when you ask for copies as models for other students.

- Identify and date each grade you enter in your grade book. Some teachers also leave spaces between students' names in order to record any additional information such as book numbers. You might also consider color coding grades as you enter them, thereby identifying daily assignments, major tests, writing assignments, and group work. If you want to eliminate the traditional grade book and design your own recording system, form 2.5, "Grade Reporting Sheet," provides plenty of space and is useful.

2.5   Grade Reporting Sheet

Class _____   Period _____   Dates _____

CHAPTER III

Creating a Master Plan, Individual Units, and Daily Lessons

- *Designing a Year-long Course*
- *Planning Teaching Units*
- *Creating Daily Lesson Plans*
- *Team Planning and Teaching*
- *Planning for Mainstreamed Students*

Creating a Master Plan, Individual Units, and Daily Lessons

My family is leaving on a three-week trip tomorrow. Can I get my assignments?

One of our goals as teachers is to chart a sensible year-long course for ourselves and our students. In language arts, this is an enormously complex undertaking because we're responsible for such a variety of facts, concepts, and skills, and our students generally come to us with widely differing abilities, interests, and goals. Add to this unscheduled assemblies, fire drills, intercom announcements, yearbook pictures, and class trips, and one begins to wonder if it's even reasonable to envision such a plan. But, of course, it is.

You'll want to begin with a general and basic plan for the entire year. In doing so, you won't be trying to fill up your year. You probably have enough material for several years. Instead, you'll need to decide what your priorities are for the material you need to cover to avoid racing from one topic to another in a frenzied attempt to get through an overstuffed course outline. Some teachers divide their textbooks into as many daily lessons as time allows, and this becomes the course curriculum for the year. Still others designate spelling days, vocabulary days, and book report days—a kind of bits-and-pieces curriculum with little correlation of concepts or integration of reading, writing, speaking, and listening. Neither approach is satisfactory or desirable, yet many of us have organized our year in this way simply to survive.

There are really two key words to keep in mind as you plan for the school year, *organization* and *flexibility*. Both long-term and short-term planning are essential, yet plans should be neither so rigid nor so detailed that they cannot be adjusted to meet daily circumstances and, more important, the changing needs of you and your students.

DESIGN A YEAR-LONG COURSE

Create a general plan or master schedule for the year, but think of it only as a guide and be willing to revise and adjust it as you go along:

1. Keep in mind the nature of the community in which you teach, the grade level and probable interests of the incoming students, other areas of the curriculum, and the total program of your school.

2. Study the district curriculum and language arts objectives outlined for your grade level or course.

3. Scan the textbooks and other materials available to you, such as curriculum guides, catalogs and publishers' materials, and lists of materials in the audio-visual department and library or media center.

4. Record the page numbers of the sections of texts that must definitely be included in your plans for the year, and keep a second list of optional choices that might be used to supplement your first choices. Look for opportunities to integrate experiences in reading, speaking, writing, and listening. Why not, for example, integrate the teaching of the library's resources with a speaking and listening project in which students interview the librarian and present their finding to the whole class in a series of oral reports or a panel discussion?

5. Think about what's going on in the world, your state, and your community. If something strikes you, jot it down and consider how this item might enhance or augment your own curriculum.

6. Plan for variety and consider themes and activities that best fit your own temperament. If you are a less experienced teacher, it is likely you will initially follow the classroom textbooks fairly closely. As time passes some of the real fun of teaching comes from trying new approaches, new lessons, better films, new writing projects, and new group activities. One of the best ways for any teacher to maintain his or her own enthusiasm and creative energy is to try some new things each year.

7. Use a planning sheet such as form 3.1, "Year-long Planning Sheet," or a calendar to plot a general outline for the year.

3.1   Year-long Planning Sheet

Course _____

August
dates

_____week 3_____
_____week 4_____
_____

September
dates

_____week 1_____
_____week 2_____
_____week 3_____
_____week 4_____
_____

October
dates

_____week 1_____
_____week 2_____
_____week 3_____
_____week 4_____
_____

November
dates

_____week 1_____
_____week 2_____
_____week 3_____
_____week 4_____
_____

December
dates

_____week 1_____
_____week 2_____
_____week 3_____
_____week 4_____
_____

January
dates

_____week 1_____
_____week 2_____

January
dates

_____week 3_____
_____week 4_____
_____

February
dates

_____week 1_____
_____week 2_____
_____week 3_____
_____week 4_____
_____

March
dates

_____week 1_____
_____week 2_____
_____week 3_____
_____week 4_____
_____

April
dates

_____week 1_____
_____week 2_____
_____week 3_____
_____week 4_____
_____

May
dates

_____week 1_____
_____week 2_____
_____week 3_____
_____week 4_____
_____

June
dates

_____week 1_____
_____week 2_____
_____week 3_____
_____week 4_____
_____

- Note any holidays, teacher inservice days, and parent conference dates.
- Sketch in end of the quarter and semester dates.
- Plot the probable length of units and assign testing days. In many schools, attendance drops just prior to a vacation, and you may want to avoid scheduling major projects or tests at these times.
- Consider the timing of major projects. You won't want all your classes taking tests or turning in major projects on the same day. As you schedule, also keep in mind your home life and personal obligations.

PLAN TEACHING UNITS

Once you have a general plan or outline for the entire course, you'll begin designing the first weeks and the first unit of the school year. You are likely to spend time with management and get-acquainted activities in the first week or so, but you'll want to move to a more detailed teaching unit as quickly as possible. It is at this point that you'll begin to plan in earnest by unit or by month. See form 3.2, "Unit Planning Sheet."

3.2 Unit Planning Sheet

Page _____

Teacher _____ Class _____

Quarter _____ Semester _____

Week _____ Month _____

Day	**Date**	**Activity**
Monday	_____	_____
Tuesday	_____	_____
Wednesday	_____	_____
Thursday	_____	_____
Friday	_____	_____

Week _____ Month _____

Day	**Date**	**Activity**
Monday	_____	_____
Tuesday	_____	_____
Wednesday	_____	_____
Thursday	_____	_____
Friday	_____	_____

Keep these points in mind as you plan your units:

Know your students. The questionnaires and any writing your students have completed up to this point will be useful for identifying some of their strengths, weaknesses, and interests. Ideally, you should also consult and include students in the planning and goal-setting process.

Identify specific goals. What do you want your students to know or be able to do by the completion of the unit? This is important, because you need to communicate these objectives to your students.

Select your resources. What books, handouts, films, or other materials and equipment will you need?

Design the class activities. What will you do and what will the students do? What learning activities will help students accomplish the goals of the unit? Because your students will have a variety of learning styles, you will want to vary the types of activities you plan. If possible, use more than one type in each class period. You'll have a great many options to consider. For example:

- reading silently and aloud
- discussing
- listening
- role playing
- watching and responding to a film or video
- brainstorming
- listing
- mapping
- freewriting
- revising and editing
- participating in small and large groups

- interviewing
- competing in teams
- playing games
- note taking
- drafting/writing
- researching
- answering questions
- summarizing
- debating
- analyzing
- paraphrasing
- peer teaching
- conferring

Create a sequenced plan. It is a good idea to write your unit plans in general terms on a monthly calendar and distribute copies to each student. The calendar should indicate the daily assignments, the materials you expect students to bring to class each day, and the dates for tests and major assignments. By distributing such a schedule you will enable your students to practice good time management and your expectations will always be specific and clear. Many computer programs allow you to produce individualized calendars for class assignments. Form 3.3, "Assignment Calendar," is also useful.

Plan to evaluate both the students and the teaching unit. How are you going to know if the students have learned? How will you know if the unit is successful? Decide on the means of evaluation you will use to determine student learning, and make it a part of your basic lesson design. (See chapters 4, 5, 6, and 7 for a more extensive discussion concerning the evaluation and grading of reading, writing, speaking, listening and cooperative activities)

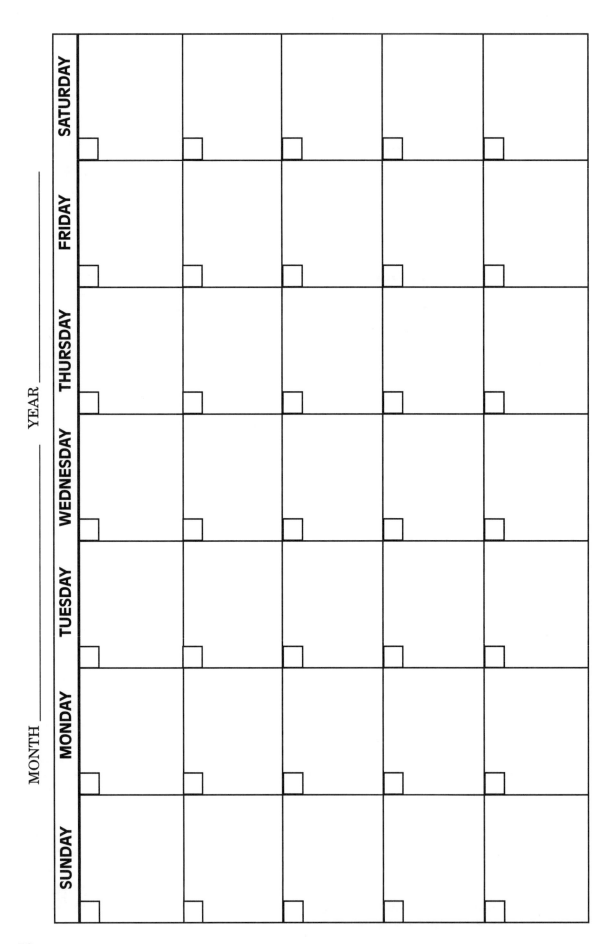

MONTH _____ YEAR _____

SUNDAY	MONDAY	TUESDAY	WEDNESDAY	THURSDAY	FRIDAY	SATURDAY

© 1994 by The Center for Applied Research in Education

Sample Unit Plan—Writing Autobiographically

The following is a ten-week writing unit designed by a teacher for a ninth-grade English class:

    1. Know your students. These students are still a little frightened by this new world—the high school. They are gregarious and social. Two are extremely quiet and shy. There seems to be a strong sense of group loyalty and a big need for peer approval. All students are reading at grade level or above. (Four are at 12th grade.) When these students write, they have little concern for editing (especially spelling) and they all seem to write in one long paragraph. Experts say students this age should be showing a growing capacity for critical thinking.

    2. Identify goals. I want to have these students begin writing and using the writing process early in this course to prepare them for the subsequent writing activities. I want to emphasize prewriting, revising, and editing as separate activities. The students will work in small groups for peer editing, using listening and speaking skills, and practicing critical thinking. I also want to structure the lessons to encourage students to write several drafts before they polish and edit the final one. Some of the elements of writing I want to emphasize are: appeals to the senses, direct dialogue, metaphor, simile, interesting beginnings, effective endings. I want to emphasize spelling, punctuation, and paragraphing as editing skills.

    3. Resources. I have lots of samples of student writing that can be used as good models. Dictionaries and thesauruses are available for each student. I can use *Dandelion Wine* by Ray Bradbury and *Growing Up* by Russell Baker as literary examples of autobiography. There is an audio tape of Garrison Keillor reading from *Growing Up* in AV. Gary Paulsen, who wrote *Tracker,* lives in our community. It would be good to have these students meet a published author. We can refer to and study any classroom set of novels when the students begin writing dialogue and when I begin emphasizing paragraphing. I can also bring some stuffed toys from home along with *The Velveteen Rabbit* when I ask them to write about one of their own childhood toys. The boys may think this topic is too babyish at first, so I want to head that off.

    4. Activities. The students will practice many pre-writing activities throughout the ten weeks: listing, brainstorming, mapping, freewriting. I can include a brainstorming game, writing, reading aloud, and working cooperatively in large and small groups to edit and revise their writing to produce a finished, polished draft.

    5. Plan and sequence. I plan to have these students write five autobiographical papers in the next ten weeks, which will ultimately be collected and bound as their own book. With each writing, I will introduce one or two new elements of strong writing and show students how to incorporate that element into their own writing. This is the sequence of elements I will introduce in each writing assignment:

***Writing I**—A Childhood Toy*
- pre-writing activities such as brainstorming and listing
- peer editing and revising
- editing for spelling, punctuation, and paragraphing

***Writing 2**—A Childhood Memory*
- appealing to the senses

Writing 3—A Childhood Friendship
- direct dialogue
- metaphor
- simile

Writing 4—An Adult from my Childhood
- an interesting beginning

Writing 5—A Time I Grew Up Quickly
- an effective ending
- editing for economy

6. Evaluation. I will design a checklist for small groups to use to respond to one another's writings, and I will use the same checklist when I respond to and grade final drafts. Students will need to know their books should have a cover, title page, table of contents, and a section about the author. We should complete these books for parent-teacher conferences, and I will need student permission to display or share their books.

CREATE DAILY LESSON PLANS

One of the drawbacks in relying on a single textbook for a course is that as we "cover" the book, it becomes easy to lose sight of what our day-to-day objectives are. Many of us have simply noted page numbers as a lesson plan for a particular day. When we do this, we have no clear focus or well-thought-out plan for what we want to accomplish. In addition, we have little useful information for another year: what we did successfully and what didn't work, for example.

It is well worth your time to use a consistent format in planning for each day. Begin by deciding on a design that appeals to you or fits your teaching style.[1] See form 3.4, "Daily Lesson Design." Duplicate enough copies of this or a similar design for every day of the year. If possible, try to plan about two weeks ahead. Fill in one sheet for each teaching day. On that day your plan will become a helpful teaching guide. At the end of the day, analyze the plan and fill in the evaluation section. What worked and what didn't? Some teachers color code these forms and write their evaluations in different color ink as a helpful reminder when they use or refer to the plans another time. Place each in a binder or folder, and by the end of the course or the year you'll have a complete and invaluable record of the year-long course, individual units, and daily lessons.

3.4 DAILY LESSON DESIGN   Name _____

Class _____

Unit _____   Lesson _____

Date _____

1. Objectives _____

_____

_____

_____

2. Materials _____

_____

_____

_____

3. Procedure _____

_____

_____

_____

_____

_____

4. Evaluation of students _____

_____

_____

_____

5. Evaluation of lesson _____

_____

_____

_____

Sample Daily Lessons

The following sample lessons are for days two and three of the ten-week writing unit mentioned earlier in this chapter. On day one, the teacher talked about and showed some of her own childhood toys, read excerpts from *The Velveteen Rabbit, Growing Up,* and *Dandelion Wine,* and encouraged students to think about some of their own childhood memories. She explained that they, too, would be writing autobiographically in the coming weeks. (A sample response sheet for evaluating the final draft of this writing is included in Chapter 5. Because objectives are focused, evaluation is simplified.)

(

Daily Lesson Design

Name _M. Jones_

Class _9th Grade English_

Unit _Autobiography_   Lesson _2_

1. Objectives

A. _Students will practice brainstorming for writing ideas._

B. _Students will focus on one idea and brainstorm for more ideas_
concerning their focused topic.

C. _Students will freewrite about one idea._

2. Materials

– _newsprint_

– _colored markers_

– _Tootsie Rolls_

3. Procedure

A. _Explain brainstorming._

B. _Organize groups of three._

C. _Distribute Tootsie Rolls, one sheet of newsprint and marker to each group._

D. _Have each group compete for number of ideas they can list about Tootsie Roll in five minutes._

E. _Individuals brainstorm long list of their childhood toys._

F. _Individuals choose one toy and brainstorm a list of details._

G. _Using the brainstormed list, individuals freewrite about toy for five to six minutes._

4. Evaluation of students

Give students time to edit briefly. Have as many as possible read their drafts to the class.
Comment on good details to the whole class following each reading.

5. Evaluation of lesson

This lesson worked well. Students had fun and came up with many ideas. Because everyone read from
his or her own desk, no one seemed threatened by reading aloud.

Daily Lesson Design

Name *M. Jones*

Class *9th Grade English*

Unit *Autobiography*　　　Lesson *3*

1. **Objectives**

   A. Students will add new detail to their writing about a childhood toy.

   B. Students will write a second draft.

2. **Materials**

   Lost-and-found section of the newspaper

3. **Procedure**

   A. Read sample lost-and-found announcements.

   B. Have students write a pretend lost announcement for each toy, emphasizing specific detail.

   C. When finished, read around room; point out good detail.

   D. Have students brainstorm a list of words they could use to describe toy to someone who is blind.

   E. Have students insert new details into first draft.

4. **Evaluation of students**

   Confer with students, asking each to point out new details he or she has added to the original draft.

5. **Evaluation of lesson**

   Students have difficulty inserting new material into an earlier draft. Plan to spend plenty of time working one-to-one with students at this point.

TEAM PLANNING AND/OR TEACHING

There are many possibilities for teachers to plan and teach together. For example:

- If your classroom is near others who are teaching similar subject matter, consider planning and/or teaching a unit together. Collaborate and tap one another's strengths, ideas, and resources. You might join forces for a research project. An auditorium or library can be used for bringing students together in large groups, and each of your classrooms could become shared learning centers or spaces for separate group activities.
- Team up with a teacher in another discipline, and base the writing assignments in your class on the content in the other area.
- Create collaborative projects with a teacher in the visual arts, or become involved in a visiting artist program.
- Create a new class entirely. For example, an American studies class might include American history, literature, and composition and involve teachers from the English and social studies departments. It might also involve collaboration with the school's art and music teachers.

PLANNING FOR MAINSTREAMED STUDENTS

More and more states are mandating the mainstreaming or *inclusion* of students with special needs in regular classrooms. Instead of going to a resource room, they attend regular classes, and a special education teacher works alongside the classroom teacher to help these students. As more students with special needs are placed in our rooms, the need for team planning will be even more evident. This will involve working with the special education teacher as well as a school psychologist, social worker, parents, other teachers, and possibly a recreational therapist. Through team planning you will have help, support, and encouragement from professionals who have the records, information, and expertise to design individual learning plans based on what each student can do. In addition, this team will include a case manager who will help you think in terms of possibilities, make adaptations in your expectations and materials, and provide follow-up support.

Although we can expect that more and more students with special needs will be mainstreamed, our classrooms already contain many who suffer from learning disabilities. This is a very broad term for students of average and above-average ability who have difficulty learning in the usual or normal way. These may be students who are mildly handicapped, students who have previously received special services, or students whose disabilities have not been identified. Many have been mislabeled as "difficult" or "discipline problems," and they sometimes arrive in our classrooms filled with frustration, anxiety, and low self-esteem. Unfortunately, they are often perceived as lazy and unmotivated. With older students, it may be difficult to differentiate between what they can do and what they can't or won't do. Having experienced so much failure themselves, they are frequently the first to call attention to the errors of others.

Pacing and Risk Taking

Students with learning disabilities have a difficult time processing language. As a teacher asks a question, the other students will already be processing an answer. However the students with learning disabilities may still be processing the question. These students have twice the processing load to do as opposed to the rest of the class. In addition, many have difficulty focusing anything out—everything gets their attention. They are not risk takers nor do they like surprises. One approach is to control and slow the pace of your classroom and to give honest praise for a good response. One teacher makes a pact with his students with learning disabilities. Because he understands that anxiety affects performance, he tells them, "I will never call on you unless I am standing in front of your desk during a class discussion." He is careful to ask only questions the student can answer. Over time the student with learning disabilities becomes confident enough to volunteer.[2]

Motivation

We frequently believe that these students are unmotivated and the key to overcoming their disability is to improve their motivation. However, motivation only enables any of us to do to the best of our ability what we are capable of doing. We're in error if we believe that if we push these students hard enough, they can learn along with everyone else.[3] The experience of many students with learning disabilities is of being the only student in a classroom who can't do something. Many have difficulty with reading comprehension, motor coordination, and oral expression.

Reading Comprehension and Class Performance

Many teachers believe that vocabulary building is the key to teaching comprehension. They reason that if readers understand every word in a passage, they will understand the passage. However, comprehension is a complex task requiring much more than the simple decoding of material. Because students with learning disabilities must put so much energy into decoding what they have read, the content is frequently lost. The following suggestions are useful in helping these students with reading:

1. Individualize reading assignments. It's especially important to give these students the freedom to choose what they want to read. If they are reading what interests them, they are more likely to gain meaning from their reading.

2. Include plenty of pre-reading discussion. Comprehension has more to do with background than it does with vocabulary.

3. Encourage students to guess words they don't know, then move on.

4. Allow students with learning disabilities to stop reading something they are not enjoying or to skip parts of a book that are too difficult.

5. When you assign a section of reading to a class, begin by surveying the material. Preview major concepts. Raise one or two questions and encourage students to read to answer the questions. Color-coding important information in textbooks helps the student with reading disabilities know what is important and what is not.

6. Encourage students to glance back to pick up what they've missed or to skim ahead to prepare for what's coming.

7. Provide extra information whenever possible. Pictures and illustrations support and confirm what a reader sees in print.

8. Provide auditory support. Make a practice of reading all directions out loud or calling on another student to do so. Many students with learning disabilities cannot understand a set of directions when they read them, but they will understand when they hear them because they need auditory input for comprehension. That's why it is important that some students hear their books on tape. They can get their information through their ears and understand it, but they frequently can't understand if they are forced to rely entirely on their eyes.

9. Give these students plenty of time to complete their oral or written responses. Many suffer from *disnomia,* a word-finding problem similar to the feeling of having a word on the tip of your tongue but not being able to say it. Most of us are capable of both associative and cognitive tasks. Associative tasks are those in which more than one thing can be done at the same time—walking and talking, for example. Cognitive tasks are those which we can only do one at a time—a mathematical computation, for example. Some students with learning disabilities are capable of only cognitive responses. They can concentrate on only one task at a time. Some may not be able to take class notes because, for them, listening is a cognitive experience, and they cannot write and listen at the same time. For these students, ask another student who can take notes to make a carbon copy. For students with disnomia, speaking is a cognitive process. For this student, begin a class discussion by asking everyone to write down several ideas in response to an opening question. After allowing for plenty of writing time, call on the student with learning disabilities first, because his or her list is likely to be the shortest.

10. Because cursive handwriting may be difficult for students with reading problems, type written assignments and handouts. If this is not possible, especially as it pertains to information on the blackboard, print legibly.

11. As you prepare worksheets and tests, keep the following in mind:
- Leave plenty of white space between sections and items.
- Avoid crowding too much information on one page.
- Include clear and concise directions.
- Use familiar terms.
- Use simple sentence structure.
- Call for one operation at a time.
- Provide examples.
- Limit the types of questions or activities.[4]

Your school's special education teacher is your single most important resource as you work with students with learning disabilities. Three especially helpful print sources are:

Chalmers, Lynn. *Modifying Curriculum for the Special Needs Student in the Regular Classroom.* Moorhead, Minnesota: Practical Press, 1992.

Tilton, Linda Kollitz. *Keymakers: A Multi-Media Based Staff Development Program for Educators.* St. Paul, Minnesota: Minnesota Association for Children/Adults with Learning Disabilities, 1988.

Lavoie, Richard D. *Understand Learning Disabilities: How Difficult Can This Be?* (video). Greenwich, Connecticut: Eagle Hill School Outreach, 1989.

As a teacher of students with learning disabilities, it is important that you not dwell on what students cannot do, but rather on what they can do—and then work to help them do it even better. Your students need you to have realistic expectations for them and a chance to succeed on these terms.

CHAPTER IV

Designing, Monitoring, and Grading Cooperative Learning Activities

- *Designing Group Activities*
- *Monitoring and Evaluating Cooperative Group Work*
- *Grading Cooperative Group Projects*

_____

Designing, Monitoring, and Grading Cooperative Learning Activities

We're all in this together.

Some students learn best through competition. Others learn best through cooperation. Still others prefer to work independently toward a goal. Consequently, you will want to keep a fair balance of cooperative, competitive, and independent activities for students in your classroom. Researchers who encourage teachers to use group work in today's classrooms point out that cooperative learning promotes greater achievement in more students, allows students to participate under less threatening conditions than in whole-class discussions and competitive activities, and encourages them to take greater risks. In addition, students working in groups gain self-esteem, exhibit increased motivation, and regularly practice higher-order critical thinking skills.[1]

DESIGNING GROUP ACTIVITIES

How often you use cooperative groups depends on how comfortable you are with the concept. Simply placing students in groups and telling them to work together does not mean they know how to cooperate or that they will do so even if they know how. Cooperative learning is not assigning a report to a group of students where one student does all the work and the others write their names on the paper. Cooperative learning does occur, however, when each member's efforts are required for the whole group's success.

If you expect to include group work as part of your year-long teaching design, it is a good idea to introduce cooperative activities early in the year and to provide plenty of practice for students as they learn to work as part of a team. The following are some decisions you will have to make as you plan for cooperative group learning in your classroom:

How many students should be in each group?

The number of students you assign to each group should be determined by the task you want each to accomplish. Large groups, small groups, and pairs are all appropriate at various times. In the beginning you will be teaching students basic social skills for group work. At this point it's best to begin with small groups of two or three students. As students become more skillful in working together, an optimum number is generally four and no more than five students. Larger groups may represent a greater range of abilities, but they also require more skill on the part of individual members to ensure active participation by each member. Initially, very few students have these skills. The size of groups may also be determined by the materials available to you as well as the time you wish to devote to each group activity. The shorter the period of time available, the smaller a group should be. Larger groups consume more time.

How will group membership be determined?

There is no single approach to grouping students for cooperative activities. The easiest way to begin, even before you know your students' strengths and weaknesses, is simply to assign them randomly to groups in one of the following ways:

- Have students count off, and then place the ones together, the twos together, the threes together, and so forth.

- Write a specific number of authors' names or the names of literary characters on the board. Students call off the names and those with the same names become members of a group.

- Distribute colored strips of paper. If you want students to form groups of four, choose eight colors for a class of thirty-two students. Cut each color into four pieces. Students draw slips of paper and join others with the same color.

Some teachers group students of similar abilities. Others devise groups of high, average, and low abilities. Many researchers recommend heterogeneous groups, if possible, because they believe this results in more elaborative thinking and greater perspective in discussing material.[2] The least desirable approach is to allow students to select their own group membership. Self-selected groups tend to be homogeneous based on ability, race, and gender. Those teachers who believe rapport contributes to the effectiveness of the group occasionally allow students the option of selecting their own groups. One variation of the select-your-own-group method is to have students list the names of people with whom they would like to work and then place each in a learning group with one person they have chosen plus others selected by the teacher. Still another option is to offer a variety of suggestions for group projects and ask students to indicate the topics in which they are most interested. Students are then assigned to groups according to their topic choice.

How long should groups stay together?

Some teachers keep cooperative groups together for an entire year or grading period. Others change membership frequently so that by the end of the course every student has had the opportunity to work with every other student in the class. Ideally, you should plan to allow groups to remain together at least long enough for them to be successful—until they complete a task or a project, for example. If at all possible, avoid breaking up groups that are having trouble functioning effectively. One of the objectives of group work is to enable students to resolve their problems collaboratively.

What is the teacher's role in cooperative learning?

As you plan for cooperative projects in your classroom, your role as teacher is a complex one. No longer will you be the "expert" at the front of the classroom. Instead you will serve as a consultant, guide, and facilitator. You will also take a less directive role as your students prove their ability to take the initiative. In addition to identifying the objectives of a lesson and making decisions about placing students in groups, you will do the following:

A. Be specific about what you expect each group to do:

- Talk and work quietly;
- Be considerate of one another;
- Share equally in the work;
- Determine a strategy or plan for completing the assigned task;
- Determine what roles (such as recorder, reporter) are needed to accomplish the task and take turns assuming these roles. (Over a period of time, each student should have an opportunity to make an oral report to the class as a whole, for example. For a more involved project, a group may decide to keep a log to record its progress. Will one student do this, or will the members take turns?); and
- Ensure that all members of the group learn the assigned material.

B. Define what it is you expect of each member:

- Attend class regularly;
- Stay with the group;
- Take turns;
- Interact with others in the group;
- Share ideas and materials;
- Give others feedback, reinforcement, and support;
- Criticize ideas, not people;
- Be responsible for their own learning and the learning of others in the group;
- Meet deadlines;
- Fulfill designated group roles; and
- Explain and elaborate on the concepts being learned.

C. Explain what each group is to produce, the time to be devoted to the work, and the criteria for evaluation:

- Is the group to produce a list, a written summary, or an oral report, for example?
- Do you expect the work to be completed in fifteen minutes, in one class period, in several class periods, or in several weeks?
- How will the group's work be evaluated?

MONITORING COOPERATIVE GROUP WORK

The Teacher's Role

Although it may be tempting to correct a set of papers at your desk while students work in groups, it's highly important for you to monitor the operation of each group. Your role is to teach collaborative skills and to provide assistance when needed. You should plan to observe groups at work and to give them feedback based on your observations and notes. For example:

- Do group members smile?
- Do they nod in agreement?
- Do they gesture?
- Do they make eye contact?
- Does one person speak at a time?
- Do they follow directions?
- Do they ask questions?
- Do they acknowledge the good ideas of others?
- Do they disagree in a pleasant way?
- Is everyone involved and on task?
- Have they shared responsibilities?
- Do they check to see that everyone understands?
- Do they take turns acting as recorder or reporter, for example?
- Have they made an effort to include everyone?

Point out what you've observed each group do well. Use the preceding list as an observation sheet and tally the number of times you observe some of these behaviors; then tell each group what you have observed. If you see possibilities for improvement, ask for suggestions from group members or offer your own solutions, at least in the beginning. Although you may be hesitant to do this with older students, you will find that they, too, will benefit from this kind of positive feedback. Many teachers omit this opportunity to guide students in their cooperative work, and it is a serious omission. Although we may take these social skills for granted, our students who have spent a majority of their classroom time working competitively or independently will have had little opportunity to develop in this manner. The time spent "processing" (discussing and evaluating) the functioning of groups is essential because you not only want each group to accomplish a task successfully, but you also want the students to maintain these skills and relationships for the next group project.

In addition to making the processing of social skills a component of every cooperative activity, you'll want to ensure individual accountability. As groups complete their work, call on one member to explain how his or her group got an answer, reached a conclusion, or produced a report. At another time check to make sure everyone in the group understands the material and agrees with the answer the group has produced.

The Student's Role

As you evaluate a group's performance it's also important that you involve students in self-evaluation. The following are useful questions which encourage groups to successfully evaluate their own work.

- What are two things you did well as a group, and what is one thing you need to do better?
- Could you describe a problem your group encountered and explain how your group solved it?
- What is something each member did that was helpful to the group?

• What is something each member could do to make the group function better tomorrow?

Questionnaires (followed by a whole-class discussion) at the end of a longer group activity also help students to evaluate their individual performance and the group performance and to encourage growth and more skillful participation in subsequent group work. Form 4.1, "Group Evaluation," is a model questionnaire, and students may complete it either individually or cooperatively.

4.1   Group Evaluation

Name _____

Group Name or Number _____

Names of members in the group:

_____   _____

_____   _____

_____   _____

Who was the group recorder? _____

Who was the reporter? _____

Were there other roles members assumed? _____ If so, who and what were they?

_____

What were your group's objectives? What were you expected to do?

_____

_____

_____

_____

_____

_____

What procedure did your group follow? _____

_____

_____

_____

_____

_____

_____

What objectives did your group accomplish? What did you do well?

_____

_____

_____

_____

_____

_____

_____

What problems did your group encounter as you worked together?

_____

_____

_____

_____

_____

_____

_____

What might your group do to improve its performance in another such activity?

_____

_____

_____

_____

_____

_____

_____

Sample unit plan for introducing cooperative learning.

Because most students have little experience with cooperative work, it is essential that you teach cooperative skills. The following is a sample lesson plan designed to introduce students to collaborative group work and to the social skills necessary for them to function effectively. The beginning exercises are simple activities intended to acquaint students with one another as well as to help them begin building a group identity. Each exercise leads to a somewhat more complex group problem. This is an ideal beginning unit because it creates a positive classroom atmosphere and climate of cooperation that is essential if you intend to include group work in your year-long curriculum.

Day 1

A. Direct each student to write his or her answers to the following directions.

  1. Write your name.
  2. Write the name of the city where you were born.
  3. Write the name of your best subject.
  4. Write the name of a difficult subject.
  5. Do you have a job at the present time or have you had a job? If so, describe it briefly. What are some good parts of the job? Some drawbacks?
  6. List three things you can do well.
  7. Name one thing your best friend doesn't know about you.

B. Ask students to use their answers as guides while introducing themselves orally to the whole class:

C. Assign students to pairs (numbering off is quickest) and have the pairs spend approximately five minutes each interviewing one another and taking notes. (At this point, if there is an uneven number of students, you should become a student's partner, because this is primarily a get- acquainted activity.) Explain that each student is to write a brief profile (based on his or her notes) which emphasizes the two most interesting items they learned about their partners. Students should also understand they will read these profiles to the whole class on Day Two.

Day 2

A. Direct the pairs from day 1 to move their desks next to one another, then call on everyone in the class to take turns reading his or her profile to the whole class.

B. Instruct each pair to draw a line down the center of the page of a single sheet of paper and at the top of both columns write "I Remember" or "I Wish" or "I Wonder" (choose only one). Have one student begin by writing an "I Remember" (or an "I Wish" or "I Wonder") statement about any memory or idea that comes to mind. The partner reads this statement and then writes one of his or her own.

C. Ask each pair to continue to add to its list. After five or six minutes, call on the pairs to read their responses aloud. After the pairs have read their lists, point out examples of positive interaction that you have observed between students and also remind students that their lists are filled with unexpected twists and pleasant surprises because they worked and wrote together.

Day 3

A. Ask individual students to draw a line down the center of a sheet of paper to form two columns. One column is to be labeled "Likes" and the second "Dislikes." Instruct students to use about three minutes to complete his or her list.

B. Direct the students to rejoin their partners from the preceding day. (If some students are absent, simply have single students form new partnerships or have them join another pair.) Ask the pairs or triads to compare their individual lists, to note anything they have in common, and to produce a new list of likes and dislikes the members of the group hold in common. Allocate four or five minutes for this activity.

C. Have each pair or triad join another pair or triad. At this point it's best if you decide which pairs should be joined. Early observation will have given you some indication of student attitudes and personalities and an intuitive sense of which students might fit well together. You will also want to combine pairs so that there is a mix of males and females and ethnic backgrounds in each group.

D. Instruct the newly formed group of four or five students to complete the following projects. Indicate they will have approximately fifteen minutes to complete their work before presenting it to the whole class during the last fifteen to twenty minutes of the class period.

   1. Using the previous brainstorming material and any new ideas, make a complete list of your group's likes and dislikes.
   2. Calculate the average height and weight of your group.
   3. Think of an appropriate name for your group, and explain its significance.
   4. Choose a reporter to present your material to the class.

E. Following each group's presentation ask students to evaluate the way their group functioned: "What did you do well?" Point out that their group lists of likes and dislikes are extensive and often contain surprising details because of their cooperative effort.

F. Explain to the students that they will be members of this newly formed and named group for the next project or for the next several weeks (depending, of course, on what plans you have in mind for them).

Day 4

A. Ask the whole class to brainstorm a list of possible problems they might encounter as they work in their groups. A list might resemble the following:

   • Someone doesn't get along with someone else in the group.
   • Not everyone in the group takes the assignment seriously.
   • Not everyone in the group does his or her share.
   • Some people in the group are frequently absent.
   • Someone in the group hates to work in groups.
   • Someone would rather be with another group.
   • Someone feels too shy to contribute to the group.
   • The group cannot complete a major assignment by the due date.

B. Direct the groups (formed on day 3) to move their desks together to brainstorm for additional ideas they might add to the whole-class list and then design a set of positive rules for their group to follow as they work together. (It's best to have only a few rules.) Be sure the groups understand they will present their lists to the class before the end of the class period. If time allows, suggest a bonus topic, such as brainstorming a list of song titles which incorporate a theme of cooperation such as "Whistle While You Work" or "Together."

C. Call on a reporter from each group to present its set of rules (and list of song titles) to the entire class and to explain the rationale for their decisions. The following is a model set of rules and could be reproduced and distributed to all students on day 5:

"Happy Together"

- Keep all comments positive.
- Encourage one another.
- Listen to one another.
- Include everyone.
- Do your share.
- Stay on track.
- Meet deadlines.

D. Conclude with a whole-class discussion of the social skills necessary to function well in a group.

Additional group activities.

You may plan any number of additional lessons to follow these beginning activities. Keep in mind that the best assignments require students to develop their own ideas and thoughts rather than simply memorize ideas or concepts from a textbook.[3]

1. Each group creates a collage that represents the group, being sure it reflects the strengths, interests, goals, and heritage of each member equitably. Upon completing the collage, the members present and explain it to the whole class. Alternatives include creating a group flag, a motto or slogan, or a time line featuring the important dates in each member's life.

2. One student in each group begins a story by writing a few sentences. He or she covers all but the last sentence, and another student continues the story again covering all but the last sentence before the next students add to the story. Finally, one member of each group reads the group's writing to the entire class.

3. Members share with the group a scary moment in their lives. The group chooses one story and writes and edits it to read to the entire class.

4. Groups brainstorm a list of fairy tales. After selecting one, the members write a new version from another point of view. For example, the witch retells "Hansel and Gretel" or the stepmother retells "Cinderella." The reporter reads the final version to the whole class. As a long-term, more complex group assignment, this project could become a choral reading or a radio play that involves every member in an oral presentation.

5. Groups brainstorm a list of questions in response to a piece of literature. Each chooses one or two of its best questions to use as the basis for their own group discussion or to submit to the teacher for a whole class discussion. If small-group discussion is used, one member summarizes the group's ideas in a report to the entire class.

6. Groups write a summary of the important ideas in a paragraph, several pages, or a chapter. For example, if all the students in the class are reading the same novel, each group might be responsible for writing a summary of one chapter or section of the book. A student from each group reports to the class as a whole. This becomes a more valuable assignment if each group is asked to relate its summarized ideas about the book's major themes or motifs.

7. Groups write a set of directions for a specific process (how to check out a book from the library, for example). Humorous topics might include: how to fail a test, how to irritate parents, how to say the wrong thing, how to waste money, how to break a promise, how to procrastinate, and how to lose a girlfriend or boyfriend.[4]

8. The members of a group research a topic. Each person is responsible for checking at least one different source and writing four or five note cards. The group writes the report together and each member is responsible for seeing that his or her information is included. For oral reports, each member takes a part and all members help one another rehearse until they all feel at ease for the class presentation.[5]

9. A group collaborates to complete a guided response sheet. For example, after a class has read *The Gift* by John Steinbeck, the teacher designs and distributes a single response sheet to each group. (See form 4.2, "Group Assignment for Steinbecks' *The Gift*.") By distributing one sheet to a group, you will encourage cooperation and also reduces your correcting load.

4.2 Group Assignment for Steinbeck's "The Gift"

The name of your group is _____

Names of group members present. Use both first and last names.

_____   _____

_____   _____

_____   _____

_____   _____

1. Brainstorm a list of words that describe Jody. (5 points)

   _____

   _____

   _____

2. Brainstorm a list of words that describe Carl Tiflin. (5 points)

   _____

   _____

   _____

3. Brainstorm a list of words that describe Billy Buck. (5 points)

   _____

   _____

   _____

4. Who is the protagonist in the story? (2 points)_____

   _____

5. What is the protagonist's problem and how is it solved? (2 points)

   _____

   _____

   _____

6. What event is the climax of the story? (1 point)

7. Diagram the various crises which lead to the climax of the story. Include the exact day and details of each. (5 points)

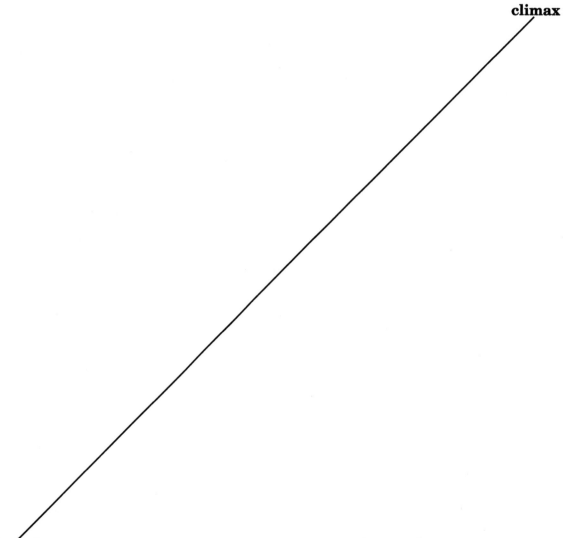

climax

Thursday

The pony is
left out in
the rain.

This activity is worth up to 25 points.

Your group's total _____

10. To ensure individual accountability, require each student to complete an assignment independently. Group members discuss and compare the work of each before submitting a single master copy for evaluation. For example, in working with *To Kill a Mockingbird,* you might ask each student to draw a map of the book's setting: the main street, the school, the business district, the courthouse, the residences of the Finches, the Radleys, Rachel Haverford, Mrs. Dubose, and Miss Maudie, and so forth. After individual maps have been completed, direct students to compare and discuss the map in groups. Finally, ask each group to produce a master map and submit it for evaluation. This is an ideal exercise because it promotes both individual responsibility and cooperation. It also prepares students for a more complex group project, such as the dramatization of a neighborhood tour (suggested in form 4.3, "Group Response Project.") Chapters 5, 6, and 7 present additional ideas for cooperative projects involving writing, reading, speaking, and listening.

It is essential that you give your students plenty of practice in learning to work cooperatively. Early practice with simple problems will allow them to gain skills such as developing brainstorming techniques, assuming positive group roles, and making group decisions—skills which will help prepare them for more complex problems later in the year. Not every effort will go smoothly, but over time students can and will improve their ability to work as a part of a team.

GRADING COOPERATIVE GROUP PROJECTS

One advantage of cooperative work is that the teacher's paper load for evaluating and grading decreases because each group generally produces a single product, report, or paper. While group assignments may be as simple as "List five questions you have about this poem," or as complex as "Produce a radio play based on the theme of this novel," grading such assignments will be much easier if you include a plan for evaluating and grading along with each assignment you design. For some, simply completing the assignment may be enough. If, for example, you ask a group to brainstorm and write five questions about a poem and to report their questions to the class, the group's grade might be based on the number and quality of questions it produces. On the other hand, major group projects which extend over a longer period of time take much more careful planning in execution, evaluation, and grading. It's best to set up rules for grading major group projects early in the year. Because student absences can disrupt scheduled presentations, criteria such as those presented below are helpful both in planning and evaluating group projects. In addition, clearly stated guidelines will promote better attendance in your classroom as students learn they are accountable to other members of their group.

Criteria for Grading Major Cooperative Group Projects

1. Each member of a group will receive the same number of points for each group assignment. Therefore, it is important that you encourage and help one another to contribute equally and to work cooperatively.

2. To receive the points you must:

- participate in planning the project; and

- participate in your group's presentation at the scheduled time. You will be given options for the dates for major assignments and presentations, and it is important that you plan ahead.

3. If someone is absent on the day of a major oral presentation, he or she loses all points. If the remainder of the group has the material and is able to make a presentation, it will be evaluated and graded accordingly. If a presentation cannot be given because a group is unprepared or students are absent, all members will lose the points. If a problem arises, consult with your group and the teacher before the due date to find a positive solution.

Form 4.3, "Group Response Project for *To Kill a Mockingbird,*" is a sample assignment for a major cooperative project in conjunction with reading a class novel.

© 1994 by The Center for Applied Research in Education

Name _____ Date _____

4.3 Group Response Project for To Kill A Mockingbird

Each of you is to work in a group to plan and present a response to this novel. Your presentations are each worth up to 50 points, and will be due on the following dates: _____

_____

Choose from the following options:

1. Each group member is to become one of the major characters in the novel. Each person writes and delivers a five-minute monologue for his or her character. Work together on writing and rehearsing the monologues to make the presentation a collaborative effort. You are encouraged to use props and costumes in your presentation.

2. Write a script for a tour conductor showing people the town in which this book is set. Describe the homes of the characters and the places where important events take place. Plan to include brief chats with the novel's characters along the way. You are encouraged to include a musical background and sound effects. This project may be taped or presented "live." Each group member should contribute to the script as well as to the taped material and to the class presentation.

3. Suppose the major characters in this book are guests on a radio or television talk show. Write and deliver an interview with the major characters. One member of the group will become the talk-show host. Other members will each become one of the major characters. All members should participate in writing and producing the script.

4. Design and produce an issue of a Maycomb newspaper following a major event in the novel. For example, you may choose to publish on the day following the trial of Tom Robinson or on the first day of November (following the events of Halloween). Each group member should contribute at least one signed story or article to the publication. Plan ahead because you may want to make enough copies of your publication for each member of the class. Involve everyone in your class presentation and be prepared to explain the steps you followed in producing the newspaper, the roles each of you assumed, and your editorial decisions.

5. Design your own group project, plan it, and have it approved by the teacher.

In planning the options for this group assignment, the teacher also designs a group evaluation form which encourages each group to evaluate its own performance. See Form 4.4, "Group Performance Self-Evaluation."

4.4   Group Performance Self-Evaluation

Name of Project _____   Date _____

Group Name _____

Names of people in group:

_____   _____

_____   _____

_____   _____

A. List the steps you followed in planning and completing your project:

1. _____
2. _____
3. _____
4. _____
5. _____
6. _____
7. _____
8. _____
9. _____
10. _____
11. _____
12. _____
13. _____
14. _____
15. _____

B. Groups of students working together are expected to encounter a variety of problems.
   Describe the major problems you encountered in completing your project:

_____

_____

_____

C. Problem solving is a skill that can improve with practice. Explain how your group solved its problems.

_____

_____

_____

_____

_____

_____

D. List the names of people in your group who were absent for at least one day of class preparation time. _____

_____

_____

E. Explain how the group and the absent individual(s) solved this problem.

_____

_____

_____

_____

F. Did you have enough class time to complete your work? _____ If not, explain how you solved this problem. _____

_____

_____

G. List the contributions made by each member of the group:

Name	Contribution(s)
_____	_____
	_____
_____	_____
	_____

© 1994 by The Center for Applied Research in Education

Group Performance Self-evaluation, continued

_____   _____

_____

_____   _____

_____

_____   _____

_____

H. List the names of the people in your group who made the greatest or best contributions to your project and explain what each did.

_____

_____

I. On a scale of 1 (low) to 10 (high) rate both your work as a group and the quality of your presentation to the class: _____ Explain your answer.

_____

_____

J. What changes would you make if you were to do this project again?

_____

_____

K. What did you learn from this project?

_____

_____

L. If this assignment were to be given to another class, what changes or improvements would you recommend?

_____

_____

Because it is important for students to understand how they will be evaluated and graded, the teacher also designs a rating scale such as the one shown in form 4.5, "Evaluation of Group Project and Presentation," and distributes it along with the assignment at the beginning of the unit. In addition, the scale reduces and simplifies the teacher's task of evaluating and grading each group presentation

4.5   Evaluation of Group Project and Presentation (50 points)

Group Name _____

Name of Presentation _____ Date _____

Names of Students in Group:

_____   _____

_____   _____

_____   _____

© 1994 by The Center for Applied Research in Education

1. *Presentation of project to the class as a whole*   (10) _____
   Does the whole class understand clearly what is being
   presented? Is each group member involved in the
   presentation?

2. *Completeness of Project*   (10) _____
   Has the group developed its project as completely as
   possible? Has each member contributed to the final
   project?

3. *Originality of Final Project*   (10) _____
   Does the group's presentation exhibit independent
   and original thinking?

4. *Mastery of Project*   (10) _____
   Is the group in control of its project or does the
   presentation appear to be an indifferent attempt to
   complete an assignment? Has the group solved its
   major problems?

5. *Group Self-evaluation*   (10) _____
   Has the group evaluated its work carefully and
   thoroughly?

Total (50) _____

Additional suggestions for evaluating and grading cooperative work.

1. For some projects, consider giving two grades—one for achievement and one for cooperative skills. In addition to grading a group's project, for example, you might also give each group a total number of points for its group work. Have the group decide how the points will be distributed. It must be a team decision on who earns what points.

2. Provide group awards. Suppose a group works together during the week in preparation for taking individual tests. Award bonus points if every member of a group achieves a specified number of correct answers. If everyone scores 75 percent or above, for example, give five bonus points to each team member.[6] You may want to evaluate academically handicapped students according to specialized criteria so that other group members are not penalized. This option is perfectly acceptable and students will welcome and support this decision.

3. Have students work independently to complete a study sheet or to answer a set of questions. Then have the members work in a group to certify that each person's work is correct. Pick one paper at random, grade it, and award all group members the same score.

4. If at all possible, don't allow cooperative work to lower a student's class average. Offer alternative independent assignments for students who are absent.

5. Group work in conjunction with long-term reading assignments can be particularly frustrating if some students are unprepared. One approach is to tell students they cannot work in a group if they have not completed the necessary preparatory work. Without being judgmental or punitive, suggest they read or work quietly in a corner while the students who are prepared to work in groups do so. Assure everyone you will provide the same or alternative assignments to individuals when they are sufficiently prepared to complete them. (This isn't as much work for the teacher as it sounds, because in most cases, individual students can be given the same assignment as that given to a group.) This is a fair approach, and students view it as reasonable. Students who do the assigned work either cooperatively or independently are rewarded. The progress of the class is not impeded by its least prepared member. Most important, over time, you will see more students completing assignments promptly because they come to view cooperative work as both productive and enjoyable. They will also understand that their work in groups is often better than that completed independently.

Grading students in their cooperative efforts often raises concern among teachers and parents, especially in relation to students who are gifted. The fear is that one student's academic progress is being sacrificed so a slower student can learn. Of course, you will want to balance your curriculum so every student has plenty of opportunity to work independently, competitively, and cooperatively. However, the bright student who excels academically but who cannot work with others in a social setting is equally deprived. The "real world" values negotiation and cooperation. Health-care personnel consult one another. Advertising executives brainstorm and coordinate sales campaigns. The automotive industry promotes team effort. Every student in our classrooms can and will benefit by learning, practicing, and using cooperative skills.

CHAPTER V

Teaching Writing

- *Teaching the Writing Process*
- *Managing Your Writing Classroom*
- *Using Mini-Lessons*
- *Sharing Student Writing: Presenting and Publishing*
- *Evaluating and Grading Student Writing*
- *Designing Assignments for a Variety of Formats*

Chapter V

Teaching Writing

If "The Sun" is too big a topic, could I write about the moon?

The teaching of writing has undergone a quiet revolution in recent years. More and more secondary teachers are adopting the process approach and writers' workshop in their classrooms. If you have wanted to use this approach but have wondered how to begin, this chapter will help you do just that. If you have already introduced elements of the writing process in your classroom, you will find many additional ideas and suggestions for refining your approach. Perhaps you prefer another approach entirely. Many of the ideas and suggestions included in this chapter will be helpful to you as well. There are a variety of successful approaches to the teaching of writing, and the suggestions offered here are intended to help every teacher be an effective teacher of writing, to help you reduce your paper load, and to help you encourage your students to become active participants in their own writing and learning as well as the writing and learning of their classmates.

TEACHING THE WRITING PROCESS

The process approach to teaching writing views writing as a recursive process involving many steps: planning, drafting, discussing, revising, editing, and sharing the results.

Prewriting.

This is a time of preparation before writing the first draft. It helps writers generate and explore ideas and is critical to the success of the entire writing process. By introducing a variety of prewriting activities, you can help your students discover many ideas for their own writing topics. (Options for a variety of prewriting activities will be discussed later in this chapter.)

Drafting.

A completed writing usually involves several drafts. In the earliest draft, the student begins by quickly jotting down ideas in rough form. It is a time to gather, explore, and discover ideas without worrying about neatness or correctness. Not every draft will be taken through the entire writing process, and those which are undergo further revision and refinement in subsequent drafts.

Revision.

Revision is the re-seeing of a piece of writing. Once a first draft is completed, a writer becomes concerned with the effect of the writing. Early changes may involve ideas and their sequence. The writer deletes material that doesn't belong and adds to or keeps what is strong. Later drafts are concerned with rearranging, reforming, and unifying the piece as a whole. Sentences may be combined and paragraphs adjusted. A final revision involves proofreading, polishing, and editing. Not all writers work alike, but by emphasizing writing as a several-stage process, you can help your students become successful writers.

Presenting/publishing.

This is the stage frequently omitted from school writing. Students have generally written only for the teacher. Today, we encourage them to write for and deliver their writing to a variety of audiences. This may include reading aloud in class, in a group, or in another public forum, turning in a piece of writing for evaluation to you, delivering it to someone outside the classroom, displaying it, or submitting it for publication.

Encourage your students to work as nearly like professional writers as possible. Although you may suggest subjects, help them discover their own topics and expect them to write in a variety of forms for a variety of readers. Confer often with your students and encourage collaboration in small and large groups. Your students will revise and edit their work when it counts most—before submitting it to you as a final draft for a grade.

Common Concerns about Teaching the Writing Process

But what about teaching the basics? Shouldn't my students complete the grammar book before moving on to writing? Students do need to master certain skills. These are best taught, however, in the context of writing, primarily during the revising and editing stages, rather than through isolated exercises. The revision stage is the time when the most learning about writing occurs, and it's important that you elicit several drafts from students when you expect them to carry their writing through the entire process. Rather than teaching the grammar book from cover to cover, use it as a helpful resource for mini-lessons as your students revise and edit their own writing. (Mini-lessons will be discussed later in this chapter.)

Will my students be prepared for competency tests—the SAT, for example? More and more of these tests require students to prepare a writing sample. Because your students will write frequently and produce many kinds of writing, they are likely to be more versatile and fluent than students who have not done so. In addition, their experience with revision and proofreading prepares them for objective questions that require them to detect and correct errors.

Having my students write more will take time. How can I possibly do all this and still teach literature and speaking and listening? Current research encourages us to view both reading and writing as processes which are naturally compatible. Although some writing may be taught independently, writing may also be a pre-reading activity, an activity during reading, and one of many possible responses following reading. (See Chapter 6 for a discussion of a variety of responses to literature.)

Researchers point out that students who write about what they read remember more and read more critically. Their reading scores improve and their vocabularies expand.[1] In addition, collaborative group work with both reading and writing encourages students to practice listening and speaking skills. Your planning and successful classroom management will allow you to create a classroom which successfully combines reading, writing, listening, and speaking. It is possible for you to teach all the elements of language arts effectively and well.

MANAGING YOUR WRITING CLASSROOM

There is no single approach to teaching writing, but planning is essential. At times you will plan for whole-class activities. At other times your students will work independently or in small groups. Use whole-class instruction when you:

- introduce a new prewriting activity;
- discover the whole class needs a particular lesson in mechanics;
- want to give everyone essential information;
- want to involve students in solving problems or setting up procedures; or
- want the whole class to listen to students' writing.

If you want to keep the entire class together through an entire writing, try the following schedule:

Day 1: Introduce a prewriting activity to help students discover a variety of possible topics, then narrow these options to a more focused topic and generate additional ideas concerning the topic.

Day 2: Plan to have students use the entire class period for writing a first draft based on their ideas from day 1. (Although most writing happens in the classroom, students may continue to work on their drafts outside class.)

Day 3: Students rework their drafts in any way necessary to share with classmates on day 4.

Day 4: Students meet in peer groups to share their writings with classmates and to respond to the writing of others.

Day 5: Introduce a mini-lesson. The type of lesson will depend upon the element of writing you wish to emphasize. It's best to concentrate on only one or two concerns rather than trying to cover everything.

Day 6: Students revise and produce a more polished draft. Student-teacher conferences **occur at any time throughout these days, especially as students move to more polished drafts. (Student-teacher conferences will be discussed later in this chapter.)**

Day 7: Students proofread individually or in pairs and begin a final draft.

Day 8: Students complete final versions to present to a particular reader.

You may plan for a single writing or a unit project which includes a series of related writings. Introduce or emphasize one or two new elements with each new assignment. The following sample plan is an autobiographical unit, previously mentioned in

Chapter 3, designed by a teacher for ninth-grade students (although it could be used with other age groups as well). This teacher plans for a variety of prewriting activities based on broad, general themes. Instead of trying to teach everything about writing in every assignment, she will introduce and focus on one element at a time (such as appealing to the senses or using direct dialogue). Earlier get-acquainted writings have indicated that her students have difficulty with paragraphing and that they need help in editing for spelling and punctuation. These elements become the focus for editing in each paper in the series. Finally, she plans to have the students collect and bind their five final polished writings as personal booklets at the end of the unit.

A sample writing unit.

Writing 1: A Childhood Toy. The students will be introduced to brainstorming, listing, and freewriting. They will produce several early drafts to fuse into a single, more polished writing. Finally, they will work in peer groups to edit for spelling, punctuation, and paragraphing.

Writing 2: A Childhood Memory. This writing will focus on appealing to all five senses. The emphasis on editing will continue to be spelling, punctuation, and paragraphing.

Writing 3: A Childhood Friendship. The emphasis will be on direct dialogue as well as spelling, punctuation, and paragraphing.

Writing 4: An Adult from My Childhood. This paper will be concerned with an effective beginning as well as spelling, punctuation, and paragraphing.

Writing 5: A Time I Grew Up Quickly. An effective ending will be the focus of this writing. In addition to spelling, punctuation, and paragraphing, the students will edit for economy.

Planning for Many Types of Writing

Although we encourage students to choose their own topics and formats, it's unrealistic to think they will try all kinds of writing without guidance. Most students prefer expressive writing and personal narrative, and you won't want to discourage this because this type of writing builds fluency in young writers and underlies all other kinds of writing. You may want to begin with expressive writing early in the year, but you'll also want your students to write in a wider variety of forms as the year goes on. The terminology used to classify writing can be confusing. Sometimes writing is classified according to purpose, sometimes according to form and style. The four modes of discourse are often called narration, description, exposition, and persuasion, and these terms are found in many textbooks today. Another classification, based on both purpose and audience, can be helpful as you plan for a variety of writing formats.[2]

Expressive writing is loosely structured and exploratory. Journals, diaries, logs, informal personal essays, informal letters, brainstorming, freewriting, short reaction papers, personal narratives, reminiscences, and memoirs encourage this kind of writing.

Formula writing is highly structured and conforms to standardized forms such as letters of appreciation, sympathy, congratulations, and application; business communication; invitations; résumés; jokes, riddles, and fables.

Imaginative writing is intended to delight and entertain and places its emphasis on language and plot. Students writing in this way produce songs, tales, poems, myths, jokes, riddles, stories, anecdotes, essays, or letters.

Informative writing emphasizes subject matter and is intended to explain or clarify some content to a reader. Reports, reviews, letters, advertisements, research papers, examinations, essays, newspaper articles, profiles, and observations encourage this kind of writing.

Persuasive writing is intended to influence the reader's point of view. Students writing persuasively may produce reports, editorials, letters, research papers, advertisements, or essays.

Prewriting Activities

Ideally, your students will choose their own topics and define their purpose and audience. We teachers have commonly used class discussion, listening, observation, research, or field trips as activities prior to writing. Other highly effective prewriting techniques will also help your students generate writing ideas.

Brainstorming. This technique is intended to generate as many ideas as possible about a subject. Although students may brainstorm independently, interaction in groups is an especially effective way to gather many ideas and to view a subject from a variety of viewpoints. Generally, the teacher leads such a session, but you may also want to encourage students to be leaders. Begin with a stimulus—a word, a phrase, a picture, or an object. Some teachers use the (volunteered) contents of students' pockets as stimuli for a brainstorming session. The leader asks open-ended questions, probes for more complete responses, and then asks more open-ended questions. In brainstorming there are no "wrong" ideas or suggestions. Record every answer or appoint a student to record them.

Listing. A variation of brainstorming is listing. The leader encourages students either independently or in a group to make long lists of ideas about possible topics. This often revolves around a common theme such as "List as many of your childhood toys as you can recall." Once students complete their lists, they choose one item on the list that interests them and that seems to have possibilities as a writing topic. Then they make a second extended list of details and ideas concerning that single item. (Other list topics might include: "How to . . . ," "Things I Know," or "Things I Would Like to Know.")

Listing in response to questions. Students list in response to questions designed by the teacher. Questions for a prewriting exercise in preparation for writing a memoir might resemble the following:

1. Make a list of people who have been important in your life.
2. From this list choose someone who would be a good subject for a writing, someone you'd like to write about. Write that person's name below your original list.
3. How would you describe this person to someone who does not know him or her?
4. List several places you remember being with this person.

5. List several things (pictures, songs, clothing) you associate with this person.

6. What feelings do you have when you think of this person?

7. List several incidents involving this person.

8. Look over your list of incidents and underline the most interesting, memorable incident.

9. Look over all the ideas you have jotted down and circle material that pertains to the incident you have underlined.

10. Using the underlined and circled material as a reference, begin writing a memoir of your special person. Focus on a single incident involving the two of you.[3]

Clustering or webbing. Clustering is a nonlinear brainstorming activity that generates ideas, images, and feelings around a stimulus word such as the following example based on the word *toy.*

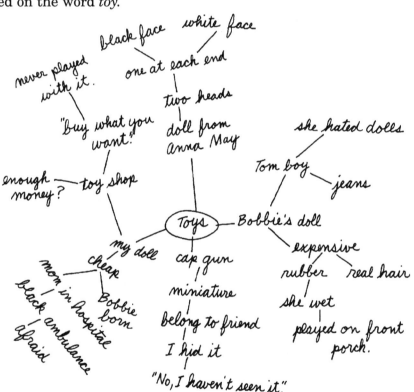

In listing, the writer usually connects ideas to a preceding word in the list. Clustering, on the other hand, allows connections to be observed and recognized in a variety of directions across the page. Introduce clustering to students by first modeling it on the blackboard. Circle a single word or phrase and ask students to contribute as many ideas as possible. Write down all the student responses (radiating outward). Next, have students work independently, choosing their own nucleus word. Encourage the students to cluster as long as possible. Some researchers encourage writers to cluster until they experience a sense of direction, a conviction "you have this to write about."[4] Successive clusters can help writers narrow a topic that is too general. *Mind-mapping* is a term often associated with clustering or webbing. It is used more often to organize material that students have brainstormed earlier. For example:

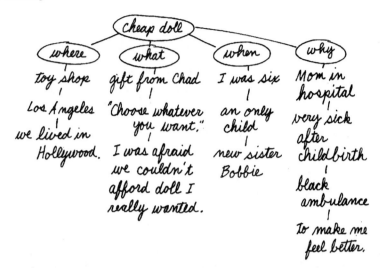

Freewriting and focused freewriting (rushwriting). Freewriting is stream-of-consciousness writing. The writer begins by putting down whatever comes to mind as quickly and impressionistically as possible without rereading, pausing, or editing. When writers slow down or get stuck, they keep their pens or pencils moving across the page, writing the same words or phrases over and over until something else comes to mind—and it will. The goal is to generate a variety of ideas. Freewritings are usually short and intense and are usually timed from three to ten minutes. Focused freewritings are written in response to a general idea or topic, but it's perfectly acceptable for the writer to move in other directions. The following is a sample prompt for a focused freewriting:

> Accidents can be good or bad, and we've all had them. Think of an accident you have had. Have you ever broken a bone, been hurt in a car, met someone unexpectedly, accidentally? List some possibilities on your paper. Choose one idea and freewrite about this accident.

Rehearsing. After students have completed a prewriting activity and have found possible topics for writing, they work in pairs, taking turns discussing their ideas and clarifying the plan each has for a writing. The student's partner listens carefully so he or she can paraphrase what was said. You may have the students explain their plans a second time to another partner or to the class as a whole. Talking about writing prior to the actual drafting helps students focus and clarify the topic and purpose of their writing.

Drawing. This technique is frequently used with young writers, but it is equally as effective with older students. Students may simply be asked to draw a picture before writing. This could be a response to an idea, a depiction of a locale, a sketch of a still life or a single object. Some teachers give students objects from a desk drawer and ask them to draw the objects before writing about them. This is an ideal prewriting activity for a poem, for example. In drawing, the writer must really look at the object, and the sketch may serve later as an illustration to accompany the final draft.

In a variation of this activity and as a preparation for writing a short story, one teacher asks each student to find a picture in a magazine of an interesting face. The students are instructed to attach their pictures to a sheet of blank paper and to place these inside a school locker door or on a dresser mirror. Mentally, the students are to take their characters with them wherever they go—to the mall, to an after-school job, to a basketball game. What would this character buy? What would he or she say? Whenever an idea occurs to the writer, he or she jots it down in the blank space surrounding the picture. In this way, the student begins to create the protagonist for a story. Students may also be asked to draw a floor plan for the character's house or a map of the character's neighborhood, or clip out a wardrobe for the character from a magazine. From here, students may have their characters "meet" in letters, telephone conversations, or face-to-face encounters. Student writers create an antagonist in the same way. Later, students brainstorm for a setting and conflict and, finally, they write their short stories.[5]

Mapping. Mapping as a prewriting activity can be used in a variety of ways. Students might be directed to draw a map of a neighborhood, a classroom, or a trip, for example. The following is a sample set of directions for mapping a childhood room.

1. Take out two sheets of paper. On the first, draw an outline of the room you slept in when you were young.

2. Pretend you can look down on your room. Label eight or nine things in that room. (If you can't remember, make some up.)

3. Write a 1 on your map where there is a window. On your second sheet of paper write the number 1, and tell me what you see from the window.

4. Suppose you're playing a game with someone in the room. Write a 2 on your map where this is happening. On your second sheet of paper write the 2 and describe a game you played. (If you didn't really have a game, what did you have to do?)

5. Write a 3 on your map where some scary sounds are. On your second sheet, tell about them.

6. Write a 4 on your map where this thing would be: something you loved the most (this may be an object or a feeling). On the second sheet of paper, tell me what it is like and why you care about it so much.

7. You're being punished (you may be innocent). Write a 5 on your map where you would go in the room. On the second sheet of paper tell what you are accused of and how you feel about it.

   At this point, the teacher asks for suggestions from students about what other details might be added to the map. Additional ideas include:

   • something under the bed
   • a pet in the room
   • objects on a shelf or a favorite book
   • someone in the doorway saying something important

8. Mark two places on the map that seem most interesting.

9. Find a group, no smaller than three, no larger than four, and explain your two items to the rest of the group. The group members may ask you questions about your ideas.

10. Finally, pick one idea to write about and begin a draft.[6]

An activity such as this is ideal. It helps writers generate many ideas. It also encourages them to focus and choose their best option and requires them to try out these ideas on an audience.

Visualization (guided imagery). Visualization encourages writers to travel mentally to another time or place—to an imaginary locale or to a real memory—to discover specific details and sensory images. You act as a guide to help students create pictures in their minds. The following is a sample set of directions for a memory exercise.

> Today, we're going to do a visualization exercise. As I turn off the lights I'd like you to relax at your desks and close your eyes. Now I'd like you to pretend you are looking at a movie of your life. Let the images flow as you look for moments in your life that appeal to you as a writer. [Pause.] Recall a time that is important to you. Perhaps it's a time when you are unbelievably happy or a time when you are sad or afraid. Pick one memory and replay the images. See the memory again. [Pause.] Look at the scene carefully. Where are you? What is happening? Examine the details of your surroundings. Find a detail you have forgotten. Now, move on. What do you look like? What are you feeling? What are you doing that shows this? Are there other people in your memory? If so, what are they doing? Look at them carefully. Listen carefully. What are the sounds you hear? What do you smell? Watch this movie in your mind for as long as you want, and when you are ready, pick up your pen or pencil and begin writing.

Idea starters or prompts. Students may find ideas for writing in films, field trips, poetry, and guest speakers or from set prompts. For example:

- Show students a picture or a series of pictures and have them create a story based on what they see.

- Give students a short vocabulary list and have them work in groups to use each word in a story.

- Distribute copies of a poem (or have students choose one) and "translate" it into a newspaper article, a personal letter, or a television news report. You might also bring in short, quirky news stories from magazines or newspapers and ask students to rewrite them in a new format.

- Read the opening lines of a story and ask students to create their own version from that point on ("Tonight I'd like to dream about . . . ," "Tonight I'd be afraid to dream about . . . ," "Be quiet, the whole neighborhood will hear . . . ," or "Turning the corner . . . ."). Or supply concluding sentences, such as "We just smiled at each other," "I did it," "Suddenly, everything went black."

- Bring a collection of interesting "junk" to class (old eyeglasses, an empty aspirin bottle, a few coins, a torn ticket stub, for example) and ask students to create a character who might own this junk. Use the collection as a basis for writing a character sketch or inventing a story. If students are to work in groups, each group may be given a separate collection. Reading a story in which an article of clothing has special significance is a good follow-up activity (the fur piece in Katherine Mansfield's "Miss Brill," for example.)

- Gather several travel posters and write haiku in response to the poster.

- Examine the travel section from several newspapers and ask students to write about their own neighborhoods as a tourist attraction.
- Read newspaper weather reports and write a script for a TV weather person or read the "letters to the editor" section and write a letter in reply to one.
- Study a dog training manual or driver's license handbook and rewrite a rule as a poem.
- Select several pages from a popular teenage novel and adapt them as a screenplay or radio play.
- Examine a copy of *Who's Who in America* and write an entry for a friend or someone students have interviewed.
- Use set prompts such as the following:
  - Not all inventions or discoveries have been good for the world. Write about one the world would be better off without, explaining why.
  - Some people feel high school students should not work at after-school jobs. Take a position on this issue and state the advantages or disadvantages of working after school. What effects do these jobs and the long hours have on students? Give supporting reasons.[7]

Interviews. Give students plenty of classroom practice in interviewing:

- Practice interviewing one another.
- Write and distribute a short biography of yourself, and ask students to write interview questions based on your handout. Then let them interview you.
- Bring someone into the classroom for a whole class interview and have students collaborate in writing a paper based on the interview.
- Expect your students to write on a topic that will require them to acquire information from other students, teachers, parents, or community people. For example a student might interview other students and a counselor about the difficulties of having divorced parents. Another might interview a doctor and students about an eating disorder. Still others might interview their parents and teachers concerning the changes in their school in the last fifteen years. (The success of Eliot Wigginton's *Foxfire* books has inspired many teachers to initiate student interviews with older members of their community. One approach is to have students read stories from the past; then each interviews a resident of a nursing home, collecting information and anecdotes to create a story. Finally, after writing, revising, and editing, the students return to the nursing home to read their stories to a gathering of the residents.)
- When students have completed a writing project, ask them to interview one another about their papers and include the interviews as well as the writings in a class publication.

Journals. Many teachers ask students to write in a journal notebook several times a week. (This may be coordinated with a reading journal. See Chapter 6.) Some expect students to discover their own topics. Others provide suggestions, such as the following:

- What is the quietest sound you know?
- What is the noisiest racket you've ever heard?
- Write a note that is going to be put in a bottle and dropped into the sea.
- Describe yourself as a friend would describe you.
- Write about a simple pleasure in your life.

The journal provides a risk-free setting for writing practice and for experimenting with and exploring language and ideas. In addition to *The Diary of Anne Frank* and *Walden,* display other published books based on the journal format. Students enjoy the following, for example:

- *Robin's Book: A True Diary,* by Robin Miller (1986, New York, Scholastic): a real-life twenty-one-year-old cystic fibrosis patient's personal journal.

- *Beyond the Divide,* by Kathryn Lasky (1986, New York, Morrow): written in journal form about the westward expansion in North America from the point of view of a fourteen-year-old Amish girl who travels west with her father in search of a new life.

- *Be True to Your School: A Diary of 1964,* by Bob Green (1987, New York, Atheneum): a well known *Chicago Tribune* columnist's true chronicle of his junior year in high school.

- *The Amazing and Death-Defying Diary of Eugene Dingman,* by Paul Zindel (1987, New York, Bantam Books): a fictionalized account of a boy's summer job.

Journals have become so popular with teachers there is a danger of their being overused. If this is the case in your school, consider requiring students to keep a more focused journal for a shorter period of time. For example, ask students who work before or after school to keep a journal of their work experience. Then expect them to develop at least one entry into a more polished writing. (A work journal might extend to research concerning nutrition and fast food.) An assignment such as this helps students see the value of a journal in discovering and developing their own topics. Still another option is to assign a travel journal for those students who are away from school for a family vacation.[8] See form 5.1, "A Travel Journal."

Name_____ Date _____

5.1   A Travel Journal

You're making plans for travel. While you're away, we'll be thinking of you and looking forward to hearing about your journey. Complete this travel journal and plan to share it with your teacher and classmates when you return.

Background:

1. Where are you going?

2. What is the reason for this trip?

3. When did you begin making preparations?

4. Who will accompany you?

5. How will you travel (car, airplane, boat)?

6. What is your itinerary? List it here:

7. Have you been to this location before? Explain.

8. Make a list of the clothes you plan to pack.

9. In addition to clothes, what else do you plan to take with you?

10. Don't forget a good book! List the titles of books you expect to take along.

© 1994 by The Center for Applied Research in Education

11. Have you encountered any problems so far? If so, describe one and explain how you solved it.

12. What are you most looking forward to during the time ahead?

13. Draw or trace a map of your trip. Plot your route in red.

Day One

_____   _____
day   date

Weather: _____

1. Schedule of activities:

   a. _____

   b. _____

   c. _____

   d. _____

   e. _____

   f. _____

2. In a paragraph, describe some of the features of this location: land, plants, animals, climate, for example.

3. Write a poem focusing on the sites and sounds around you.

Day Two

_____   _____
                day   date

Weather:_____

1. Write a paragraph describing as completely as possible your room at this location. Include a rough sketch—for example, the size of the room, color of walls, floor covering, windows, beds, closet, ceiling fan, air-conditioner, phone, television, or radio. You might also include a description of the view from a window.

2. What are the best known towns or cities in the area you are visiting?

3. What are the best known historical sites in the area? What makes them notable?

4. On the back of this sheet, staple or paste a post card or pictures cut from a travel brochure. Explain each in a sentence or two.

Day Three

_____   _____
day   date

Weather: _____

1. Compare and contrast this location with home. Begin with a brainstorming chart:

home		vacation spot
1.	1. language	1.
2.	2. food	2.
3.	3. clothing styles	3.
4.	4. recreational activities	4.
5.	5. people	5.
6.	6. sounds	6.
7.	7. smells	7.
8.	8.	8.
9.	9.	9.

Write your paragraph here:

2. On the back of this sheet, sketch something you did or saw today. Include a sentence or two explaining your sketch.

Day Four

_____   _____
             day   date

Weather: _____

1. People-watching is always fun. Describe at least three people who have caught your attention. Include both a physical description and an explanation of what they were doing.

    a.

    b.

    c.

Day Five

_____   _____
                    day   date

Weather: _____

1. Make a list of the unusual or exotic foods you have eaten.

2 Make a list of the most memorable events so far.

3. Choose one item from the list above and write a letter on the back of this sheet to a friend at home, describing this event in detail.

Day Six

_____   _____
day   date

Weather: _____

1. Schedule of activities:

    a. _____
    b. _____
    c. _____
    d. _____
    e. _____
    f. _____
    g. _____

2. In a paragraph, describe the best or worst part of this day.

3. Time is slipping away. What will you miss most about this spot when you return home?

4. What will you miss least?

© 1994 by The Center for Applied Research in Education

Day Seven

_____   _____
day   date

Weather: _____

You have decided to develop your travel adventure into a major motion picture. You will be the producer as well as the author, so you'll have to begin making plans. Complete the form below:

1. List the cast of characters needed for this film:

2. Decide which well-known actors you will hire to play these roles. Write their names alongside the cast of characters above.

3. Where do you plan to make this movie?

4. List the major scenes to be included in your movie. These should be based on real events.

   a. _____
   b. _____
   c. _____
   d. _____
   e. _____

5. List five possible titles for this film. Circle your first choice.

   a. _____
   b. _____
   c. _____
   d. _____
   e. _____

6. What rating would you give your movie?

7. On the back of this sheet, sketch a poster advertising your movie.

Day Eight

1. You've returned home. Think about all you've done and seen on your travels. What advice would you give someone planning to visit the same location?

2. Evaluate your travel journal.

3. Would you recommend a journal for anyone else who is planning to travel? Explain.

4. Which entry might you use as the basis for a more formal, polished writing?

5. What changes and revisions would you make to your entry to polish it?

Helping individual students get started.

Despite a variety of excellent prewriting activities, some students may still have trouble initially in getting anything down on paper. Try asking questions about what he or she is considering. Then repeat the student's answers and ask for amplification. Echoing the student's words builds confidence and gives him or her the first lines to begin writing.

Not every student needs prewriting activities such as these, but some will find them useful. Most important, avoid an inflexible approach that leaves little room for individual learning styles or modes of expression. Give students many options and allow them to recognize and use what works best for them.

Handling painful topics.

If your students write often, sooner or later you will encounter a paper about a painful topic. If the paper recounts physical or sexual abuse, you must report it. The law is clear. It's important, however, that you decide beforehand how you will handle such an occurrence. Many teachers explain to their students that if a particular writing makes the teacher fear for their safety, the teacher *must* do something about it. Most students who write in this manner are signaling for help and are usually willing to seek a counselor or proper agency if encouraged to do so. If at all possible, avoid using a student's writing as evidence, or at the very least, seek permission to do so.

There are many painful subjects students write about that need not be reported. You must be prepared to respond to these in a healthy way as well. It's important to understand that the act of writing out something that has caused pain is itself a therapeutic act.[9] Students who write personally about painful topics are dealing with these problems in a healthy way. Respond with empathy but don't try to become the student's therapist. If the writing is submitted "for your eyes only" maintain the student's privacy and confidentiality. However, painful topics can have an enormous effect on an audience if they are shared aloud with the whole class. Some students will do this, although, of course, you must never require it. Again, it's important that you keep your response in perspective. If you spend an inordinate amount of time reacting to inflammatory topics and less time with more ordinary topics, other students will feel the need to write in a confessional mode. No student should feel pressured to do so, but those who do should feel that freedom as well. Balance is important.

Student-Teacher Writing Conferences

Student-teacher conferences, one-to-one discussions, may happen at any time in the student's writing process. They may be informal and impromptu as you move around the room from student to student pointing to strengths in a writing, giving honest, specific praise, and answering questions. Ideally, you should respond as a reader, not as a teacher (or expert, or judge, or literary critic). This is called an "I-referenced response." Each time you make a comment, precede it (at least mentally) with the phrase "When I read this, I . . ." For example, "When I read this part, I feel . . .," "When I read this part, I see . . .," "When I read this, I get confused about . . . ."

Researchers tell us a reader's response is more useful and less threatening for students than any other kind we can make. I-referenced responses help students pay attention to the elements in their writing in ways that help them develop their writing further.[10]

Student-teacher conferences may also be formal and planned. Some teachers schedule formal conferences before or after school, during lunch periods or prep periods and have students fill out sign-up sheets or appointment cards. However, there is only so much time in a teacher's day. It's preferable to hold these meetings during class time in a quiet corner of the room when the other students are at work. You may schedule a block of days for formal conferences or fit them in as your students' needs and the schedule allow. For writing which is to be carried through the entire process, you should plan to meet briefly with a student several times through a series of drafts. At the prewriting stage, conferences may simply consist of offering suggestions for a focus or helping a student discover more details or information. Ideally, conferences will be concerned with only one or two features of a writing at a time. Comments concerning editing and proofreading are reserved for later drafts. Formal conferences are most successful when they follow a predictable routine, even to the extent of asking the same questions to begin each conference. The following set of questions provides a useful format for a formal conference. Questions such as these will allow you to see the writing through your students' eyes and keep them responsible for it.[11]

1. What would you like me to listen for (or read for) and react to? (If time allows, student should read aloud because confusion about meaning and syntax often disappear when they do so.)

2. What part of your draft do you like the best?

3. What part gave you the most trouble?

4. What would you like to change in the next draft?

5. What have you learned from writing this draft?[12]

Unfortunately, the tendency for many of us is to assume the initiative in a conference to the point of becoming active collaborators in a student's writing.[13] One of our goals as teachers is to help students become independent writers. It's important to remember that during these conferences the student should be doing most of the talking, and we should be listening. Write on students' papers as little as possible. Show them how to solve problems, but do not do it for them.

Formal conferences with student writers may appear to be difficult and time consuming. However, once established and practiced, your students will become more articulate about their own writing. In addition, your response will be immediate and meaningful and far more helpful and effective than red-penciling a final draft when the student believes his or her work is completed.

Keeping track of what each student is doing.

Some teachers keep a set of index cards in a file box to record formal conferences with students. A separate card is kept for each student and is available to students at any time. As you confer, write a brief summary on the front of the card, such as "Working on setting—planning to add sensory words." At the next conference review the card with the student, then go on to discuss the student's progress. You can reserve the back of the card to note skills that are being worked on. When one card is filled, staple another to it. The card will serve as a good record of the student's progress. Other teachers keep a record of formal conferences with students by using a notebook with a page for each student. The page has columns for the date, the title of the writing in progress, conference notes, and skills to be worked on and resembles the sample that follows:

	Date	Writing Assignment	Plans for Revision
		Student Record of Writing for _____	
1.			
2.			
3.			
4.			
5.			

Teachers whose students keep writing folders use separate sheets of paper to record the same information. The sheets are stapled to the inside of the folder or to the drafts of the writing itself. Keeping the notes on student's progress with each writing saves time. Your students will see evidence of their progress and will be reminded of their goals; you will be able to quickly identify the needs of each student and groups of students as you plan for mini-lessons. Form 5.2," Student Writing Profile," is also helpful as a means of charting a student's overall progress.[14]

5.2   Student Writing Profile

Student's Name _____

(Enter a check (√) if the student has any of the problems listed below.)

Writing	1	2	3	4	5	6	7
Date							
Ideas							
Organization							
Sentence Variety							
Voice							
Grammar, usage, mechanics							
many misspellings							
errors in punctuation							
errors in use of verbs							
errors in use of pronouns							
errors in use of modifiers							
errors in word usage/vocabulary							

Small-group conferences.

Peer conferences can occur with two students, small groups, or with an entire class. They will require a good deal of initial effort on your part to make them succeed. (See Chapter 4 for a detailed discussion of cooperative learning.) Despite this, peer conferences are well worth your effort in saved time and student learning and involvement. Peer groups expand a writer's audience and provide an opportunity for students to analyze and evaluate the writing of others—the kinds of thinking we teachers too often reserve for ourselves. Students must learn how to respond to the writing of others in a positive, constructive manner. In addition, working together is not a skill that most students have had practice with. Plan with other teachers to demonstrate a peer conference for several classes at one time or rehearse small group of students to demonstrate for the whole class. Peer conferences are most successful when you establish a consistent routine. Form 5.3, "Directions for Students Working in Small Groups," is a helpful format for peer conferences.

5.3   Directions for Students Working in Small Groups

Directions for the author:

1. Don't apologize for the writing.

2. Read your draft out loud just as it's written on your paper.

3. Ask question 1: "What do you like about my writing?"

4. Listen to the responses of every person in the group.

5. Ask question 2: "What questions do you have about my writing?" Wait for everyone to respond.

6. Ask question 3: "What suggestions do you have for making this writing better?"

7. Ask to have anything you don't understand clarified.

8. Thank the members of your group.

Directions for small groups:

1. Bring a draft of your paper to class on the due date.

2. After being assigned to a group, move your desks together quietly.

3. Quickly decide who will read first.

4. Listen carefully as a draft is being read. When an author is reading, no one else should be talking.

5. When asked, respond to the author's questions out loud. Do not interrupt others.

6. Remember to be kind and helpful in your responses.

7. Go on to the next author and repeat the process.

8. After every person in your group has read, continue working quietly and independently on your own revisions.

Remember, the purpose of writing groups is not to attack, criticize, find mistakes, or concentrate on surface errors. It is a time to be supportive and kind, to let the writer know that you hear what he or she is saying. Tell the writer what you like and offer suggestions for making the next draft better.

As students meet in peer conferences, encourage them to jot down their ideas as the writer reads. Some teachers have students write out complete answers before responding orally. The written response is then given to the author who refers to it when revising. Ideally, group membership remains the same as a paper is taken through the entire process. New groupings may be planned for subsequent writings. The preceding response format is based on three questions:

1. What do you like about the writing?
2. What questions do you have about the writing?
3. What suggestions do you have for making the writing better?

Some teachers use the same response format for every writing. Others design focus questions to reflect the basic characteristics of specific kinds of writing. For example, the focus questions for a fable might be:

1. Are the main characters animals or inanimate things in nature?
2. Are the personalities of the characters appropriate for what happens in the story?
3. Does the moral grow out of the story?

The focus questions for a memoir might be:

1. What is good about this writing?
2. What is the relationship between the writer and the subject of the memoir?
3. On what incident does this writing focus?
4. Could the reader point out the subject of the memoir in a roomful of people?
5. What needs to be added to this writing?

As a writing nears completion, students also help one another edit for mechanical concerns. Checklists such as form 5.4, "Editing a Final Draft," are helpful.

5.4   Editing a Final Draft

Author _____   Date _____

Editor _____

Editor   **Author**

_____   1. Are all the words spelled correctly?   _____

_____   2. Is all end punctuation correct?   _____

_____   3. Are words capitalized correctly?   _____

_____   4. Are commas where they belong?   _____

_____   5. Do all the verbs agree with the subjects?   _____

_____   6. Are the paragraph indentions where they should be?   _____

Editor's comments:

_____

_____

_____

_____

_____

There are likely to be several students in each class whose mechanical errors are beyond the help of another student. On editing days, place these students in a group to work with you.

Be prepared for some "failed" conferences, but don't give up on them. Collaborative work requires practice and patience and encouragement from you. In time, students can learn to work well together, and successful conferences will evolve.

USING MINI-LESSONS

We need to be involved with our students at every stage of their writing. Students need to learn to master certain skills if they are going to become proficient writers. These are best taught in the context of their writing rather than in isolation. At this point students have a reason for learning, and they are able to apply this learning immediately. Many teachers design mini-lessons to help students along the way, being selective rather than overwhelming students with too many activities. Mini-lessons can involve small groups of students or whole-class activities. The following are examples of the kinds of short lessons you can plan for your own classroom:

Mini-lessons for Prewriting and Drafting

Use large sheets of paper, the overhead projector, or the chalkboard to model a prewriting process such as listing or clustering. Talk as you write and explain your ideas to students. Tell about each possible topic and why it matters to you. Plan your list so you can reject one because you can't think of enough to say about it, another because it's too personal to share, or another because you don't like thinking about it right now. Explain which topic you will choose and invite students to ask you questions about it. Demonstrate another list or cluster based on the more focused topic. On another day, model your own drafting process. Demonstrate that early drafts are hurried and chaotic as a writer hurries to capture as many ideas as quickly as possible. Invite students to make comments and observations and to ask questions.

Mini-lessons for Revision

Don't expect students to revise every writing. Instead, spend more time on some pieces, and teach your students how to revise. Many don't see the possibilities for change. Others are satisfied with neat drafts and are reluctant to make changes. Some teachers counter this by asking students to write early drafts on only one side of a sheet so that they might cut them apart and move sentences or paragraphs around. One teacher rewards revision efforts by offering a "messiest draft of the week" award. It's important that students understand that revision is separate from drafting. Students should write on one day and revise on another, if possible. Consider using one of the following mini-lessons to acquaint your students with revision and to give them practice in responding to one another's writing.

Introducing revision.

1. Display on bulletin boards drafts and revisions of student papers. Include the messy first drafts as well as the final copy. Read papers written by former students as models, and make plenty of student writing, bound in handmade booklets and anthologies, available for students to read. Let them see and read the result of thoughtful revision. Show how much pride you take in the polished work of previous students.

2. Use the overhead projector to demonstrate as you revise one of your own papers or show the changes a former student has made in several drafts of a writing.

3. Practice with the whole class in responding to writings. Find copies of several drafts of a single writing by a previous student. Duplicate copies for everyone. Hand out the first draft and ask students to read and respond to it using the same format they will use in their peer groups. ("What do you like about this draft?" "What questions do you have?" "What suggestions do you have for making it better?") Unfortunately, students often feel they are expected to find only what is wrong with a writing. Dispel this notion. Help them look for the strengths first. Teach students how to make helpful responses to writing. Force them to be specific and to explain why they answer as they do. "It's a good story" isn't a helpful response, but explaining what makes it "good" is. ("The verb *clattered* helps me hear the sound.") Students need to be encouraged to examine texts carefully. After the class has arrived at suggestions for making the draft better, hand out the second draft and go through a similar response. ("What is still strong?" "What has improved?" "What could make it still better?") Lessons such as this early in the year will help your students better understand how they should respond to writing in their peer groups and will also help them begin to form their own definition of effective writing.

4. After students have worked in peer groups for a time, ask them to write a paragraph about a particular response or the kind of peer response that is most helpful to them personally. Ask them to analyze and explain the changes they have made from one draft to the next.

5. Display a transparency of a student paper on the overhead. Ask the students to respond in writing to the following or similar questions:

- What did the writer write about?
- What is strong about this writing?
- What sensory details help you imagine the incident?
- Where is dialogue used or where could it be used?
- What word choices do you admire?
- What changes might make the writing stronger?

Writing prior to a class discussion involves everyone, focuses thinking, and guarantees a stronger whole-class discussion. Consider asking students to give the model paper a grade and explain why they gave the grade they did. Grades will, of course, vary. Discuss how this can happen and why.

Revision is a highly complex process. It varies according to the type of writing as well as the age and ability of the writer. To make revising more manageable for students, some teachers break the process into several stages: adding, cutting, substituting, and rearranging. The following suggestions for mini-lessons are arranged according to these categories and the options suggested here simplify it even further. Don't expect your students to do all of these. Use them only when you see a need—even then, one or two mini-lessons per final draft may be plenty.

Revising by *adding*

1. Encourage students to expand portions of their writing. Direct them to examine their drafts and to note places that lack detail or are underdeveloped. They brainstorm, list, or cluster for ideas to expand that section. Finally, on a separate sheet of paper, they write a new version of the section to insert in a later draft.

2. If your students have access to word processors, ask them to type two consecutive sentences from their drafts onto the computer screen. Next, have them place the cursor between the two sentences (The telephone rang/She answered it). Finally, they type until the screen is entirely filled with additional ideas and details that could logically fit at that point in the original draft. (Without a word processor, ask students to write the first sentence at the top of a sheet of paper, the second at the bottom of the page and add details between the two to fill the page.)

3. Encourage students to include sensory detail by reading through their drafts and adding information about how something looks, sounds, feels, smells, or tastes.

4. Enable students to include specific information and sensory detail by suggesting they write additional short drafts in a new format or for a new audience. For example, the students' first drafts might be descriptions of an object such as a toy. After the original drafts are completed, students write a lost-and-found notice for the same object. Next, they write a paragraph describing the object to someone who is blind. Finally, they underline the specific detail in all three versions and incorporate the best details into a new draft.

5. Ask students to add surprises and comparisons. Are descriptions fairly ordinary? Is the snow always white, the sky always blue, the night always scary? Have groups brainstorm for surprising ways to describe snow (scarred by a North Dakota wind), the sky (green as mold), and the night (shivering in northern lights). Finally, ask students to examine their own drafts to add surprises or comparisons.

6. Suggest the addition of direct dialogue. Examine an author's use of direct dialogue in a familiar novel or short story:

- How does it differ from indirect dialogue? (She said that she was happy. / She said, "I am happy.")
- What do quotation marks tell the reader?
- What are dialogue tags, and does the author use them?
- How do we know when the speaker changes?
- What rules has the author followed in using quotation marks?

Next, ask students to study their own drafts and mark one or more places where direct dialogue might occur. Finally, on a separate piece of paper write a scene of dialogue which might be inserted into the original draft. When the dialogues have been completed, students exchange papers and check one another's writing for accurate use of quotation marks.

Sometimes it's useful to ask students to write a piece completely in dialogue. After such an exercise, they will use direct dialogue more frequently in other pieces of writing. Suggest scenes such as the following:

- You are at a bank and witness an attempted robbery. The teller is hard of hearing.
- You overhear a "funeral service" that two children conduct for a dead pet.

- Two passengers in a canoe encounter stormy weather.
- You have driven your parents' car to the mall. When you return to the lot, you discover the car has been sideswiped. You drive the car home, and your parents meet you at the door.

7. Rewrite a draft from a new point of view. (The description of a toy might be rewritten from the toy's point of view.) Students compare and add the best new material to the earlier draft. (A similar activity requires students to write in a new verb tense—from past to present, for example, or change the level of language from formal to informal to slang. How might a justice of the Supreme Court describe his or her memory of a toy as opposed to a description by a professional thief?)

8. Change point of view and audience. In preparation for this, review the events of the story "The Three Bears" or a similar, familiar tale. Ask students to retell the story from another point of view and to a different audience. Papa or Mama Bear might retell the incident at work or to a next-door neighbor, Baby Bear relates his version to a playmate, or Goldilocks explains what happened to the police. If students are writing in groups, each group works with a different story. (A logical extension of this activity is to ask students to write three versions in addition to their original piece: one for a close friend, another for a stranger, a third for a parent.)

Students also enjoy reading children's literature based on this concept and you may want to share samples with them to demonstrate how changes in point of view, characterization, and setting can alter the outcome of a story. For example:

Prince Cinders, by Babette Cole (Putnam, 1987)
Snow White in New York, by Fiona French (Oxford University Press, 1990)
The True Story of the 3 Little Pigs! by A. Wolf, by Jon Scieska (Viking, 1989)

9. In a second draft the writer adopts a new mode. A narrative might become a persuasive piece, a description of one place might become a comparison of two. The new details this produces may be added to the earlier draft. The new mode may be a stronger writing. Perhaps it should be the next draft?

Revising by *substituting*

1. Consider word choices by having students white out or erase every fifth word in a paragraph or paper, number the blanks consecutively, and then exchange these papers with a partner. On a separate sheet, have a partner supply words in the blanks based on the context of the paper. This will help an author look at the writing in a new way.

2. If your students aren't already using a thesaurus, encourage them to do so. Explain the format thoroughly and then write several lines from a familiar story on the chalkboard. "There was an old woman who lived in a shoe. She had so many children she didn't know what to do." Students rewrite these lines using no words with the letter *o.* If they can't think of new words or phrases, they consult a thesaurus. Students have fun with this exercise, and although the resulting sentences may be awkward, the exercise forces them to become familiar with this resource. Next, students study their own drafts and underline words they think are imprecise and search for better choices. (If your students are using word processors, be sure they understand and use the thesaurus feature as well as the spelling checker.)

3. Help your students to use specific, active verbs. Consider the sentence, "The girl walked down the hall." Discuss how many changes a writer can effect in the reader's perception of the girl by changing the verb *walked*. What verb could make her young? Old? Heavy? Angry? Afraid? Beautiful? Sneaky? Also consider the sentence, "The boy cut the leather." Think of as many verbs as possible which would be more precise than the verb *cut*. Finally, have students examine the verbs in their own drafts and substitute active, precise verbs for any which are weak.

4. Substitute precise adjectives. Consider sentences such as the following: "His shoes were unusual." "She wore strange glasses." "The cat was ugly." "The day was unpleasant." "The road was dangerous." Groups brainstorm for better descriptions to share with the whole class. ("He wore red and pink high tops." "Her glasses were rhinestone-studded half-moons." "The scrawny, one-eyed cat." "The temperature was 40 below, and the wind howled all night." "The road was filled with unmarked potholes and strewn with fallen branches.") Finally, students make similar additions in their own drafts.

5. Direct an author or peer editor to circle repeated words lightly in pencil and connect the circles. Students will realize they need to find context-appropriate synonyms for the repeated words.

6. Help students avoid monotonous sentence patterns by underlining the first four words in each sentence in a rough draft. Study the patterns. Does every sentence begin the same way? If so, can some of them be varied to provide greater interest? (Another option is to count the words in every sentence and on a second sheet of paper draw lines equivalent to the number of words (as in a bar graph). Are all the sentences the same length? Which ones can be changed or combined?)

Revising by *rearranging*

A writing rarely begins in its final arrangement. The beginning is the most important part of a piece because it has to "hook" the reader's attention. The ending is the next most important part, because it must leave the reader with some thing to remember. The middle of the piece should tell more about the beginning and be filled with good details and examples. Sentences sometimes need rearranging too.

1. Read and discuss interesting introductions or opening sentences by published authors. For example:

- "When he was nearly thirteen, my brother Jem got his arm badly broken at the elbow." *To Kill a Mockingbird,* by Harper Lee (Harper, 1960)
- "The Herdmans were absolutely the worst kids in the history of the world. They lied and stole and smoked cigars (even the girls) and talked dirty and hit little kids and cussed their teachers and took the name of the Lord in vain and set fire to Fred Shoemaker's old broken-down toolhouse." *The Best Christmas Pageant Ever,* by Barbara Robinson (Avon, 1973)
- Where's Pap going with that ax?" said Fern to her mother as they were setting the table for breakfast. "Out to the hoghouse," replied Mrs. Arable. "Some pigs were born last night." *Charlotte's Web,* by E.B. White (Harper, 1952)

Suggest that a good introduction might open with a question ("Have you ever wondered how you'd survive without a cent?"); open with an announcement ("This is not a story for the timid"); open with a bold and challenging statement ("Contrary to what some people think, most learning takes place outside the school."); open with a quotation from somebody ("'You'll be sorry you ever asked,' he whispered."); open with a personal experience ("I'm glad I didn't cry in front of him."); or open with how the writer felt ("My chest hurt, my legs ached, and I itched all over."). Ask students to work to improve the beginning of their own drafts.

2. Change the chronology. Recall the story of Cinderella. Write the line, "The prince slipped the glass slipper on my foot," on the chalkboard. Then ask groups or the whole class to collaborate in retelling the story with the new beginning. Next, students underline an important detail in their own draft and move at least a mention of the detail to the beginning of the draft. Finally, they write a new draft based on the restructured chronology.

Revising by *cutting*.

When students write their early drafts, they are working for quantity. Before a draft is completed they will want to get rid of anything that doesn't really add to the writing. You'll have to convince them that length does not necessarily determine the quality of a writing. They are used to being told to "write a five-hundred-word essay."

1. Examine the first and last sentences of a draft. Can these sentences (or more) be omitted?

2. Write sentences similar to the following on the chalkboard. Students revise them for economy before examining their own drafts or the drafts of their peers.

- He heard it make a sound of scratching. (He heard a scratching sound.)
- The girls were runaways, and they took a bus to go downtown. (The runaway girls took a downtown bus.)
- The flowers were picked by a man who was growing flowers for a living. (The florist picked the roses.)

Mini-lessons for Editing

1. Each day select a sentence containing common errors and write it on the board. Ask students to discuss and explain corrections orally.

2. Present a lesson dealing with a critical editing skill, such as comma splices. Use a grammar book or worksheets if necessary, and then ask students to examine and edit their own writing. This may be a whole-class exercise or a small-group exercise for students who share the same problem.

3. Involve all students in a class practice. Duplicate a sample paper with numerous mistakes in spelling, capitalization, punctuation, and usage. Students work independently or in groups to improve their proofreading skills.

4. Have students read their drafts backward, from end to beginning, from right to left to check for spelling errors.

5. What do you do if you're required to "cover" the grammar book? One option is to assign each group of students a single concept—a part of speech or a rule for capitalization or punctuation or usage. Expect the group to learn the concept, study a handbook or grammar book, prepare it for presentation, develop worksheets or an assignment, and administer a test. Exercises such as this might be repeated several times throughout the year in order to cover the required grammar material. A plan such as this is an effective approach because it involves much more than the mastery of isolated skills. Your students will be reading, listening, speaking, writing, editing, and evaluating.[15]

SHARING STUDENT WRITING: PRESENTING AND PUBLISHING _____

There are a variety of ways for your students to share or publish their writing. Consider some of the following for your own classroom:

1. Students read their completed work to the whole class.

2. Meet with another class and read to one another. Older students write stories, fairy tales, legends, and myths to share with younger students. Bind these writings in booklets and donate them to the elementary library.

3. Plan a formal reading occasion (an author's tea, for example). Send invitations to guests (parents, principals and other administrators, school board members, students and teachers from other classes, a reporter from the school newspaper or the community newspaper).

4. Read to interested community groups.

5. Post writing on a bulletin board or in a display case outside your classroom, in the hallways, in the school's offices, in public libraries, or in waiting areas of a hospital or doctors' or dentists' offices.

6. Feature a "writer of the week" in a display case. Include samples of the student's writing, a picture, an autobiographical sketch, and questions and answers from an interview (or a complete interview written by a classmate).

7. Students send messages, letters, or notes to other students, administrators, school board members, family members, sports figures, political figures, business people, media figures, or civic groups.

8. Present copies of final drafts as gifts to adults outside the classroom: parents, grandparents, former teachers, or anyone else the author admires.

9. Students produce a final copy of their "best" writing on a word processor. Add a title page and bind all copies or laminate them and deliver them to the school librarian. Be sure the copies are catalogued and featured as new acquisitions. Send a second, unbound copy of this writing along with a supportive note to the parents of each student. (Explain to the students beforehand that you plan to do this.)

10. Publish each student's best writing in a handmade book or collect the writing of all students in handmade class anthologies. Include a table of contents and title page. Add sections such as "About the Authors" and "Advice to Writers." Make copies for your classroom, for gifts, for the media center, for nursing homes, or for waiting rooms and offices.

11. Produce a class newsletter or magazine with samples of student writing and mail these to parents, administrators, and school board members. (You may

want to include an editorial in which you comment on what you have been teaching or are going to teach next.)

12. Write articles for and submit student writing to a schoolwide newsletter that is sent to all parents in the school district.

13. Collaborate with students and teachers in another discipline. For example, write poetry in language class in conjunction with a science unit on insects. Publish this collection and share it with students in other classrooms.

14. Submit final drafts to the school newspaper, the yearbook, a school literary magazine, or to a local newspaper.

15. Produce a class magazine or newsletter featuring a theme of local community interest ("ecology in our community," or "the future of our community," for example). Seek out a variety of resources, including interviews with members of the community. Involve the local media and distribute the completed publication or arrange to have it published within a community newspaper.

16. Collaborate with other English faculty to select and publish exemplary student writing produced in response to English class assignments by students at every ability level. This might also be expanded to feature outstanding samples of assigned writing from all the disciplines.

17. Submit student writing to publications that accept manuscripts from young writers. For example:

American Poetry Review
401 South Broad Street
Philadelphia, Pennsylvania 19147

English Journal
Spring Poetry Festival
Box 112
East Lansing, Michigan 48223

Merlin's Pen (grades 7–10)
98 Main Street
East Greenwich, Rhode Island 02818

New Voices
1102 Buterville Road
New Paltz, New York 12561

Poetry Society of America
15 Gramercy Park
New York, New York 10003

Scholastic Magazine
50 West 44th Street
New York, New York 10036

Seventeen
320 Park Avenue
New York, New York 10022

Writer's Digest
9933 Alliance Road
Cincinnati, Ohio 45242

Youth Magazine
Room 1203
1505 Race Street
Philadelphia, Pennsylvania 19102

Writing
Curriculum Innovations
Suite 2100
60 Revere Drive
Northbrook, Illinois 60062

"Stuff You Wrote"
Sassy
230 Park Avenue
New York, New York 10169

In addition, *The Market Guide for Young Writers,* by Kathy Henderson (Shoe Tree Press, Belvidere, New Jersey 07823), is updated annually and provides a complete description of a wide variety of publications and contests that accept manuscripts from writers aged eighteen and under.

EVALUATING AND GRADING STUDENT WRITING_____

You will want your students to write frequently, but you are concerned about time. How can you possibly read and grade everything your students write?

Assignment Design

The key to easing the burden of grading student writing (especially if you expect to grade individual papers) may be found in carefully designed writing assignments. As you plan an assignment, begin with a clear idea of what it is you want your students to learn and what the student must do to achieve this goal. An assignment such as "Write a short paper that is related to this week's reading" is ambiguous. However, "Write a haiku reflecting your understanding of the theme in the book *Night* to share with your classmates at the beginning of class tomorrow" is better because it provides a student with a definite route through the assignment.

If possible, all major writing assignments should be given in writing. Ideally, each will be duplicated and distributed to every student. (You might also write these assignments on a chalkboard and expect the students to copy them in assignments notebooks.) It's best to give these assignments in a consistent format such as the following:

1. the topic
2. the speaker/writer
3. the purpose
4. the audience/readers
5. the format (or options)

All major assignments should include deadlines and final dates as well as an explanation about how the writing will be evaluated. The following is a sample assignment based on the personal essay about a childhood toy mentioned earlier.

Assignment for a personal essay: "A Childhood Toy"

1. Assignment: Write a personal essay about a childhood toy.
2. Speaker: You will be the speaker describing a toy you once owned and loved.
3. Purpose: Make your audience "see" this object and understand why it was special.
4. Audience: Your classmates.
5. Format: Three- to five-paragraph personal essay.

Important dates: We will spend _____

with prewriting (listing), drafting, and revising activities (combining several drafts)

Your rough draft is due for peer evaluation on _____.

Your final draft is due _____.

Your final draft will become a chapter in your end-of-the-unit autobiography. Give your essay a title and write (or type) neatly on one side of your paper in blue or black ink. This assignment is worth ___ points and will be graded for:

1. specific detail;
2. appeal to the senses (sight, sound, touch, taste, smell);
3. paragraph development;
4. correct punctuation; and
5. correct spelling.

A clearly written assignment such as this sample not only lets students know what is expected of them but also helps parents understand what is happening in the classroom.

Be clear about your expectations for final drafts from the beginning of the year. Form 5.5, "Instructions for Final Drafts," is one that can be posted in the classroom or distributed to each student.[16]

Name_____ Date _____

5.5 Instructions for Final Drafts

1. Head each paper in the following manner:

   _____*Title (on first line, centered on page)*_____

   _____*(blankspace)*_____

   _____*The first word of each paragraph should be indented and the second line should*_____

   *begin at the margin line.*_____

2. Capitalize the first and final word of the title and all other words in the title except articles, conjunctions, and prepositions with fewer than five letters.

3. Use only regulation-sized paper, $8\frac{1}{2}$; inches by 11 inches.

4. All final drafts should be written in blue or black ink or typed neatly, clearly, and legibly.

5. Write on only one side of the paper.

6. If your paper does not have the left-hand margin marked, establish a margin of about one inch and adhere to it closely. On the right side, leave a margin of about one inch and keep it as even as possible.

7. Indent the first word of all paragraphs uniformly.

8. Do not use the sign & or the abbreviation *etc.* Remember *a lot* is two words.

9. Divide a word only at the end of a syllable. Words of one syllable may not be divided.

10. Always reread your final draft and correct errors in punctuation and spelling (with correction fluid if necessary) before handing it in.

11. Your name should be included on your draft in the following manner:

Student self-evaluation.

As part of your lesson design, you will want to involve students in self-evaluation. One way to do this is to ask them to evaluate their writing by responding to a checklist. An ideal checklist has two characteristics: first, it is designed for a specific writing assignment; second, it distinguishes between revising and proofreading. The following is a sample student checklist designed to accompany the preceding assignment:

Student Checklist for Personal Essay: "A Childhood Toy"

Name _____ Date _____

Revision

1. Do I include specific detail in several well-developed paragraphs?
2. Do I appeal to several senses? (sight, sound, touch, smell, taste)

Proofreading

3. Does my writing have several paragraphs, and is the beginning of each indented?
4. Is my punctuation correct?
5. Is my spelling correct?
6. Is my copy neatly written on one side of the paper (in blue or black ink) or carefully typed?
7. Did I include a title at the top of the first page?

A checklist such as this encourages the student to become a part of the evaluation process and can be used for peer evaluation as well.

Teacher's scoring guides.

The information in a well-designed assignment sheet is easily converted to a teacher's scoring guide or analytical scale. Rather than undertaking the enormous task of responding to everything about a writing, you will be able to concentrate on those skills which are the focus of the assignment quickly, efficiently, and fairly. The following is a sample scoring guide for the preceding assignment.

Sample Scoring Guide

Student's Name _____   Date _____

Assignment: Personal Essay: "A Childhood Toy"

Revision

    1. The writing includes specific detail
       in several well-developed paragraphs.   2 4 6 8 10

    2. The writing appeals to several senses.   2 4 6 8 10

Proofreading

    3. The writing has several paragraphs and
       the beginning of each is indented uniformly.   1 2 3 4 5

    4. The spelling is correct.   1 2 3 4 5

    5. The punctuation is correct.   1 2 3 4 5

    6. The final draft is neatly written in blue
       or black ink (or typed neatly) on one side
       of the paper.   1 2 3 4 5

    7. The writing has a title.   1 2 3 4 5

Total Points (45) _____

Additional comments:

An analytical scale designed for each kind of writing according to its own terms is also effective as a teaching tool and will help your students better understand the characteristics of these types of writing. A description (such as that of the toy) is graded according to its clarity and focus (does the writing reveal what the writer sees, hears, smells, feels, and tastes?) and its use of language (does the writer use exact words and language that shows rather than tells?). On the other hand, a letter could be graded by rating its "voice"(does it sound as if a person is talking?) and its form (does the letter use the correct heading, greeting, and closing?).

It is also possible, although less desirable, to use one self-evaluation sheet (and grading scale) for most student writings. Such a scale emphasizes general features such as content, order, style, punctuation, grammar, and spelling and might resemble form 5.6,"Self-Evaluation Sheet."

5.6   Self-Evaluation Sheet

Content

1. My paper has a clear purpose or makes a point.
2. I use specific details and examples to help my reader understand what I am saying.
3. I omit details that are not important to my main ideas.
4. I have thought about my topic carefully and I know what I am talking about.

Order

5. I've started my paper in an effective way. The reader will want to keep reading.
6. I've told things in an order that makes sense, and it is easy for the reader to follow what I am saying.
7. All the details in my paper fit together and contribute to my main point.
8. My paper ends well. It doesn't stop suddenly or drag on too long.

Style

9. This writing sounds like me.
10. This paper shows how I feel and think about this topic.
11. It's easy to picture what I'm talking about. My words show the reader what to see.
12. I've tried saying some things in a new way. I've had fun with the language.
13. My sentences are clear and no words are left out.
14. My sentences have variety. Some are longer than others, and they do not all begin the same way.

Editing

15. I've read my paper over. It's smooth and easy to read.
16. I've proofread my paper and corrected spelling, punctuation, and capitalization.
17. My paragraphs begin in the right spots, and I've indented them correctly.

If you plan to grade individual papers, do not grade everything a student writes. Grade only finished papers that have been carefully revised and presented to you as final. Sometimes students will hand in anything to meet a deadline, and we have often graded these papers too early. Don't hesitate to return a paper to a student and ask that a revision be completed before assigning a grade. You may reduce your grading load even further by having students choose one final draft from among several for a formal grade.

Holistic Grading of Student Writing

If it is necessary for you to grade the final draft of each major writing assignment, holistic grading is another valid time-saving approach for you to consider. In holistic grading, a procedure for sorting or ranking written pieces, content and form are considered, but the tallying and marking of errors is not required. Holistic grading is helpful in assigning grades fairly quickly, but it is not useful in showing a student or parent the strengths or weaknesses of a piece of writing.

In the simplest form, the teacher reads the first paper, then reads the next and decides whether it is better or worse than the first. If it is better, it is placed on top of the first. If it is worse, it is placed underneath. The scoring or placing occurs quickly, impressionistically. The reader continues until all papers are arranged from most successful to least successful. A grade is assigned after the ordering is completed.

Another approach to holistic grading is to match papers with another piece in a graded series or to score a paper for the prominence of certain features. Again the scoring is done quickly and is usually guided by a rubric which describes particular features of writing such as content, wording, organization, flavor, and mechanics.

Grading Contracts

Another time-saving approach many teachers use in classrooms where students are expected to do a great deal of writing is a contract system for determining grades.[17] Students agree to fulfill certain obligations in order to earn a particular writing grade. The writing grade is then averaged with points earned for other class assignments to determine the final marking period grade. Form 5.7, "Writing Contract," primarily reflects the quantity of writing a student chooses to do rather than the quality of his or her work. However, students aren't expected to work and write entirely on their own. The teacher works individually with students, reads and responds to early drafts, and devotes most of his or her time to students when it really counts—when they are in the process of writing rather than after their writing is completed. One of the best features of this sample is the variety of audiences called for. Formerly, we believed the "threat" of grades caused students to edit and polish final drafts. In this contract, the revision for publication, the expectations of an adult outside the classroom, and the quality of editing demanded by a contest are all highly effective in promoting higher final copy standards. A contract should also indicate due dates for final drafts in order to prevent students from turning everything in at the last minute.

Name_____ Date _____

5.7 Writing Contract

One of the goals of this class is to help you become a better writer. You will be asked to write frequently. You will also read and share your writing with other class members as well as the teacher. Finally, you will polish and revise some of your writing for other audiences.

To earn a grade of <u>C</u> in writing for this grading period you must:

1. Write and place three writings in your folder.
2. Revise two of these writings, and attach each revision to the earlier draft.
3. Confer with the teacher, and revise one of these revisions (#2) to include in the class booklet.
4. Confer with the teacher and revise another of the these writings (#2) to deliver to an adult outside this class.
5. Meet the following due dates:

Final draft for the class booklet : _____

Final draft for an adult outside the class : _____

To earn a grade of <u>B</u> in writing for this grading period you must:

1. Write and place four writings in your folder.
2. Revise three of these writings, and attach each revision to the earlier draft.
3. Confer with the teacher and revise one of these writings (#2) to include in the class booklet.
4. Confer with the teacher and revise one of these writings (#2) to deliver to an adult outside this class.
5. Confer with the teacher and revise another of these writings (#2) to submit as a display piece for a class exhibition.
6. Meet the following due dates:

Final draft for the class booklet: _____

Final draft for an adult outside the class: _____

Final draft for the display piece: _____

© 1994 by The Center for Applied Research in Education

To earn a grade of <u>A</u> in writing for this grading period you must:

1. Write and place five writings in your folder.
2. Revise four of these writings, and attach each revision to the earlier draft.
3. Confer with the teacher and revise one of these writings (#2) to include in the class booklet.
4. Confer with the teacher and revise another of these writings (#2) to deliver to an adult outside this class.
5. Confer with the teacher and revise another of these writings (#2) to submit as a display piece for a class exhibition.
6. Confer with the teacher and revise another of these writings (#2) and submit a final draft to a local or national contest or for possible publication.
7. Meet the following due dates:

Final draft for the class booklet: _____

Final draft for an adult outside the class: _____

Final draft for the display piece: _____

Final draft for contest or publication: _____

Please sign and return

I, _____, understand that in order to earn the grade of _____, I must and will do the following:

Date _____

Signature _____

There are many options for writing contracts. It is also possible to specify and require a variety of formats: a personal essay, a poem, a letter to the editor, a memo, an analytical piece.

If you intend to use a grading contract in your classroom, you must help parents understand your approach. They are accustomed to seeing grades and comments on most of what is written for class, and they will need to know that you will place less emphasis on grading early in a course, that you will grade fewer papers, if any, but that you will also respond to more writing in a variety of ways. (See Chapter 8 for additional suggestions for working with parents.)

Portfolio Grades

More and more teachers and schools are turning to portfolios—samples of actual school work—to help evaluate student progress. Portfolios are not the same as writing folders, which generally contain all of the writing a student has done. A portfolio may be used in conjunction with reading and speaking activities or may be used exclusively for writing. It is assembled by students and is a collection which illustrates their efforts, progress, or achievements. If you plan to use portfolio assessment, decide before you begin what you want students to place in their folders and turn this list into a table of contents. The following model table of contents is one you might consider if you plan to limit the portfolio to writing samples:

1. The first writing of the semester
2. The beginning-of-the-year writing inventory
3. A writing from early in the quarter with all drafts and prewriting materials attached as well as self-evaluation materials, peer conference notes, and teacher's conference comments (The number of writings and variety of formats will depend upon the age and ability of the particular students.)
4. A writing from later in the quarter with all additional material
5. A student-selected best writing with an explanation for this choice
6. A self-evaluation

Student self-evaluation.

Because self-reflection is such an important concept in portfolio assessment, you'll want to plan for a variety of ways to encourage your students to assess their own writing. Form 5.8, "Student Self-evaluation," is a helpful format to use in conjunction with portfolios.[18]

Name _____ Date _____

5.8 Student Self-evaluation

Writing Assignment _____

1. How much time did you spend on this paper? _____

2. Describe the process you went through to create this paper.

    a. Where did you get the idea for the paper or what prewriting activity did you use to help you explore your subject and get words down on paper? _____
    _____
    _____
    _____

    b. What problems did you have with an early draft? _____
    _____
    _____
    _____

    c. What kind of revision strategies did you use to shape and to refine your draft?
    _____
    _____
    _____

3. Analyze two suggestions members of your group gave you. First list the point and then respond to the comment. Did you agree or disagree with what they said? What did you do as a result of their feedback?

    a. Group Comment: _____
    _____

    b. Your Response: _____
    _____

    a. Group Comment: _____
    _____

    b. Your Response: _____
    _____

4. What are the strengths of your paper? What points still cause you trouble?_____

_____

_____

_____

_____

_____

_____

_____

5. What do you want me to look for when I evaluate this paper? What questions do you have for me?_____

_____

_____

_____

_____

_____

_____

6. If you were to grade this paper, what grade would you give it and why? _____

_____

_____

_____

_____

_____

_____

Additional options for self-evaluation

1. Consider having students respond to questions such as:
   - Why did you choose this format (essay, short story, for example)?
   - What pleases you the most about this writing?
   - What strategies were most effective for you as a writer as you worked on this piece?
   - What new strategies did you try? How successful was this attempt with a new technique?
   - What problems did you encounter and how did you solve them?
   - Who gave you helpful suggestions? What were they?
   - What could your peer-response group do to give you even better feedback about your writing?
   - What additional changes would you make in this writing if you had the opportunity?
   - How does this writing compare to other writing you have done?
   - What did you learn in the process of completing this writing?

2. Ask students to write a description of the phrase "best writing." Then have them pick one of their writings and show how their own best writing reflects their standards.

3. Instruct students to rank their papers from most to least effective and give a rationale for their ranking.

Plan to assess portfolios periodically, every four weeks or so, and include notes about your observations. Some teachers attach a grade to these observations or formally grade an early writing as well as a later one.

DESIGNING ASSIGNMENTS FOR A VARIETY OF FORMATS

Writing Assignments that Require Little Teacher Time

"I learned" statements—Each student writes three to five sentences stating what he or she learned during a class hour or during an experience such as a film, a presentation, or a field trip. A writing assignment such as this helps students practice making notes and summarizing. While you are putting materials away following a film, for example, students write. On the following day call on several students to read from their lists to recall and review the previous class material. These summaries increase long-term retention, and may become an ongoing journal or learning log assignment.

Memos—Students write a brief explanation to a specified reader of something they have learned to do or have done. For example, students write a memo about a class activity for someone who has been absent, or they write a memo to you explaining what they know about a topic (either before or after studying it).

Micro-themes—Students write short essay answers or summaries on index cards or half sheets of paper to a question you have posed. (Some teachers also require a one-sentence summary of the response as a heading .) Micro-themes provide good practice in preparation for writing essay answers on exams. They are fast and easy for you to respond to, and the limited space forces students to focus their thinking and to write precisely and economically. Asking students to read these aloud reinforces their learning, makes them aware of a broader audience, and allows for an immediate response.

Essay Answers

Students are frequently unsuccessful in writing essay answers because they too often overlook prewriting activities and begin drafting immediately. Teach them to approach an essay answer in a series of steps:

1. Analyze the question:
   A. Circle all direction words such as *list, compare, trace.*
   B. Underline key words.
   C. Determine the number of parts to a question.

2. Develop ideas:
   A. Brainstorm, list, or cluster.
   B. Number or jot a brief outline.
   C. Reread the question.

3. Write the answer:
   A. Restate the question as the first sentence .
   B. Write a draft using the brief outline as a guide.

4. Reread and make all changes legible and clear, if necessary, but do not recopy.

The following is a sample exercise to help students practice writing such answers:

1. Hand out two lemon drops to each student. (One is to eat immediately.)
2. Explain that they will practice writing an essay answer based on the following directions: *Define and describe a lemon drop. Be sure to appeal to all five senses in your answer.*
3. Ask students to identify the instruction words and circle them. (*Define, describe,* and *appeal*)
4. Identify and underline other key words. (*lemon drop* and *five senses*)
5. Identify the number of parts to the question. (*two*)
6. Brainstorm for ideas. A sample brainstorming list might look like the following:

lemon drop

| | definition **1** | | | description **2** | |
| | candy | | | senses | |

sight **A**	sound **B**	touch **C**	taste **D**	smell **E**
yellow	pings on desk	coarse	sour	lemon
oval	crunches	gritty	sweet	tart

7. Number or letter ideas in the order to be considered in the answer.

8. Reread the question, then write an answer using the lettered brainstorming sheet or brief outline as a guide and restate the question as the first sentence of the answer. ("A lemon drop is a piece of candy which may be described according to the five senses.")

9. After the writing is completed, students read and edit their original drafts, making neat and legible changes if necessary, but they do not recopy.

10. Call on volunteers to read their trial answers aloud and make comments on what makes them successful.

11. On the following day students write an answer to a "real" question based on material they have been studying.

Research Reports

We have long asked students to write formal research reports because we believe it is essential that they learn to gather, organize, and interpret information. They need to synthesize sources with their own thinking and to handle quotations and cite references. Formal research papers require a great deal of instruction and class time and long hours on the part of the teacher in grading final drafts. Despite our best effort, the writing produced by this kind of assignment is frequently dull and voiceless.

I-search reports.

As a result of the influence of Ken Macrorie (*Searching Writing*) and others, teachers have begun to design a variety of research projects around the concept of the "I-search." As opposed to the standard research paper in which the writer usually assumes a detached and objective stance, the I-search paper allows the student to personalize his or her search for facts and ideas. Students choose topics they care a great deal about. The final draft is a first-person step-by-step narrative of their own discovery process.

The I-search paper is generally written in three sections: (1) what I assume or imagine or already know about this topic; (2) the search; and (3) what I discovered.

Section 1: Before conducting any formal research, students write a section to explain to the reader what they think they know, what they assume, or what they imagine about their topic as well as why they have chosen it. For example, if a student were writing about teenage alcoholism, he or she might estimate the severity of the problem, create a profile of a typical teenage drinker, and explain why he or she is interested in the topic.

Section 2: Students consult useful books, magazines, newspapers, film, tapes, and other sources for information. Whenever possible, they interview people who are authorities or who are familiar with the topic. A student whose topic is teenage alcoholism would read several books on the subject as well as pertinent articles in a variety of current magazines, visit a rehabilitation center for alcoholics, attend a meeting of Al-Anon or Alcoholics Anonymous, and consult an alcoholism counselor. He or she would write about the search in narrative form (usually chronologically), documenting all sources of information and using formal footnotes or endnotes when appropriate.

Section 3: In this section writers compare what they thought, assumed, or imagined with what was actually discovered. They include some personal commentary and draw conclusions. For instance, the writer on teenage alcoholism might learn that the problem is far more severe and often begins at an earlier age than he or she believed. He or she may have assumed that parental neglect was a major cause of the problem but may find that peer pressure is the prime factor contributing to teenage alcoholism.

Bibliography: At the end of the report, the writer attaches a formal bibliography listing the sources consulted during the search.

Variations of the I-search report.

1. Students work collaboratively in a group investigation and present their findings orally as well as submitting a short paper with bibliography.

2. Students research an author or a well-known person, but the final response format is multi-genre (a poem, a news article, a dialogue, a story, a journal entry, and a letter, for example).

3. Students research a career. The final format consists of four main sections: (1) a library research section describing the career; (2) an interview section with a person working in the career field; (3) a personal experience section about spending a full day observing and working with a professional from that career field; (4) a summary of the writer's findings.[19]

4. Students research a particular time in history and then write their own historical fiction, such as a narrative, drama, or exchange of letters reflecting the same era.[20]

5. Each student chooses a year in history, researches it, and produces a newspaper with important news items of the day.[21]

Letter Writing

Pen pals have been used extensively to help students write for a real audience. An alternative approach is to pair students in two classes. Without using their real names (or identifying them only by number), they write back and forth to one another. No attempt is made to bring them together, and they rely only on a written exchange. Teachers of remedial reading students often ask teachers and counselors to become pen pals with their students. The replies are immediate and students realize that their writing matters. You can also pair students with residents of a convalescent center or members of a senior citizens center.

Comparison and Contrast Writing

There are a number of organizers that are helpful when students are asked to write comparison and contrast papers.[22]

1. Circles within circles are useful for helping students see relationships and categories. The largest circle contains all members of the class; smaller circles within the large circle contain species or individual examples.

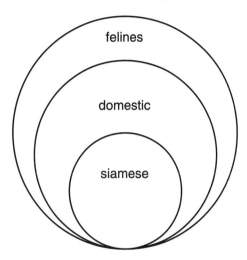

2. Venn diagrams feature overlapping circles. In the outer areas, points of contrast are written; in the area of overlap, points of similarity are noted.

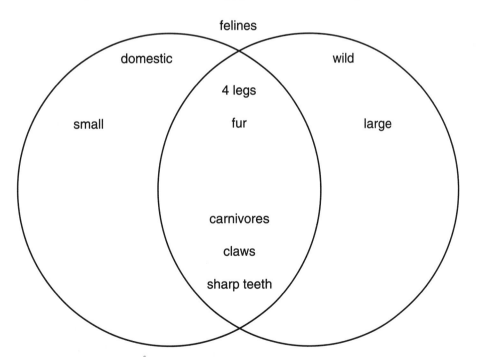

3. Ladder notes are graphic organizers which help students look at the differences between two things. The points of consideration are listed on the rungs in the middle. On one side they note the attributes of one subject, and on the other side, those of the second.

points of comparison

Calico cat_____African lion

	size	
	body	
	food	
	habitat	

Poetry

Read poetry to your students, and have them read aloud as well. Play recordings of writers reading and talking about their work. Invite a local poet to your classroom to read and talk about his or her work. Everything in poetry starts from listening to it and enjoying the experience. An understanding of a variety of formats or patterns is also helpful in initiating poetry writing with students.

Acrostic poem: The first letter in each line can be read vertically to form a word. For example:

Something
Mandatory
In
Laughing
Effectively

Students might use their own names or the names of historical or literary characters **as a starting point for their own poems.**

ABC poem: A poem with one word per line. The writer begins with any letter of the alphabet for the first word; the next line begins with the next letter of the alphabet. The poem may be as long or as short as desired, and the alphabet may be used backwards. For example:

All
Butterflies
Can
Dance

Concrete or picture poem: An idea is expressed in both verbal and pictorial form. For example:

END APARTHEID

IN AFRICA..

Cinquain: The five lines follow a distinct pattern. For example:

line 1: a one-word title	Buffalo
line 2: two words describe the title	Noble, mammoth,
line 3: three words express action	Stampeding, charging, dying,
line 4: four words express a feeling	Sadness, anger, hunger, loss,
line 5: another word for the title	Dishonored

Diamante: The seven-line poem has a specific format. For example:

line 1: one word title	Bicycle
line 2: two words describing the title	Sleek, swift,
line 3: three-*ing* words telling about the title	Pedaling, flying, soaring,
line 4: four nouns relating to the title	Wheels, pedal, chain, seat,
line 5: three-*ing* words describing line 4	Rolling, clanking, bending,
line 6: two words describing line 4	Shattered, scattered,
line 7: one word that is nearly the opposite of the title	Stranded

Wingspark: The five lines follow a specific pattern. For example:

line 1: I dreamed	I dreamed
line 2: answers the question "Who?"	Kirby Pucket
line 3: answers the question "Where?"	In the Metrodome
line 4: shows action	Hit a grand slam
line 5: describes how the action was done	Perfectly!

List poem: Any number of lines in the poem list ideas, usually without transitional phrases. List poems may be based on any possible concept (beauty, ugliness, sadness, things I like, things I don't like, untrue statements about stones or pudding). For example:

My Junk Drawer

As I struggle to open the drawer,
I find:
4 novels (unread),
20 batteries (dead),
100 feet of wire,
20 pieces of an electric train set,
1 polyester shirt I got last Christmas,
3 workbooks from fifth grade,
and the reason I can hardly open it:
clay.

Numerous variations are possible. For example: "I wanted . . . I got . . ." or "I used to be . . . now I am. . ." List poems may also repeat a word or phrase such as "every day," "don't," or "I remember."

Found poem: Lines are taken from a nonliterary source or sources such as newspapers, magazines, advertisements, labels, crossword puzzle clues, or junk mail and reshaped as a poem. For example:

original source:	found poem:

Clover Ice Cream is dedicated to perfection. We select only the highest quality, all-natural ingredients. Clover Ice Cream contains no preservatives, artificial flavors, stabilizers, additives, or colorings. This commitment to quality is why Clover Ice Cream is the finest in the world	Dedicated
	  to perfection
	Highest quality artificial
	  flavors, stabilizers,
	  additives . . .
	     finest in the
	world.

Clerihew: A humorous four-line rhymed verse, usually about a famous person, whose name is the first line. (Students might be asked to write a clerihew about themselves, using their own names.) For example:

Willard Scott
Is not
As fat
As all that.

Haiku: A three-line unrhymed poem with seventeen syllables (5,7,5), usually using present tense verbs. For example:

Goldfish in a bowl
Darting, circling, hurrying
Without arriving.

Variations:

tanka: five-lines with syllables arranged in a 5-7-5-7-7 pattern

lanterne: five lines with syllables arranged 1-2-3-4-1

septolet: seven lines with a syllable pattern of 1-2-3-4-3-2-1

Free verse: This unrhymed poetry may have any number of lines. It has no definite rhythm but is shaped on the page in a manner which gives the reader clues to its meaning. Line breaks are of particular importance. Lines can end at the end of a sentence, at the end of a phrase, or in the middle of a sentence or phrase. Words placed at the end of the line have the greatest impact. Shorter lines and white space are used to slow a poem, longer lines speed it up.

Sample prompts for poetry.

There are many, many possibilities for prompts which are helpful as prewriting exercises for poetry. For example:

1. Make a long list of words naming emotions (or any other concept—a driving test, for example). Choose one of the words from the list and make as long a list as possible of words, phrases, ideas, specific details, or incidents associated with this focus word. Include all or some of this material in a free verse poem about the topic.

2. Answer questions leading to a poem:

Line 1: What is your favorite kind of tree?
Line 2: What does this tree look like (color, shape, height)?
Line 3: What does this tree do when there's a heavy wind?
Line 4: What does this tree look like on a very dark night?
Line 5: What is the object in line 4 doing?

> Birch tree,
> Slender and white.
> Waving to the sky,
> A shivering ghost,
> dancing in the darkness.

It is possible for a teacher to create a set of questions for a variety of topics; for example:

Line 1: What is your favorite season of the year?
Line 2: What objects do you think of when you think of this season?
Line 3: What colors come to mind?
Line 4: What smells or sounds do you associate with this season?
Line 5: What activities are children involved in during this time of year?
Line 6: Adults?
Line 7: How does the weather change at the end of this season?
Line 8: How do you feel at the end of this season?

3. Directions for a variety of topics are also useful prompts. For example, directions leading to a free verse poem based on a journey might resemble the following:

A. List as many possible journeys as you can think of—journeys that might take you only a few minutes to complete (to the teacher's desk, from the car to the house, from the hall to the principal's office, for example).

B. Underline one idea that seems to hold the best possibilities for writing.

C. Brainstorm a list of people who might be making this journey.

D. From this list, pick one person and give him or her a name.

E. List as many reasons for the journey as possible.

F. Choose one.

G. List, using precise detail, all the sights, sounds, and smells your character might encounter on his or her journey.

I. Using as much of this brainstormed material as you wish, shape your ideas into a free verse poem. For example:

Tommy T's First Triple

Tommy T had hit his first triple,
A pitch down the center of the plate.
He swung his Easton, snapped his wrist
and smacked the ball into right center.
Tommy T had hit his first triple.

He raced to first, and the coach waved him on,
"Go to second, Tommy, go to second!"
Faster and faster raced Tommy
around second and straight for third.
The centerfielder hurled a long throw to short.
"Here," called the third baseman,
but Tommy T knew he had hit his first triple.

His cleats churned the sand.
He slid
as the shortstop's relay
hissed behind
The tag.
"Safe!"

Tommy T dusted
his uniform.
He had hit his first triple.

Form 5.9, "Directions for a Found Poem," is helpful as students write found poetry.

Name _____ Date _____

5.9   Directions for a Found Poem

A found poem is a poem you create by:

    (A) finding words or phrases in another piece of writing; and

    (B) arranging them in such a way that they become a poem.

Found poetry helps you discover the possibilities of ordinary language.

1. Begin with interesting prose. For example:

   - textbooks
   - notices on bulletin boards
   - classified ads
   - obituaries
   - menus
   - magazines
   - letters
   - highway maps
   - junk mail

Don't use other poetry or song lyrics or anything that has already been arranged on a page such as commercial advertising.

2. Select a section of the prose—the part that seems to offer the most possibilities. Lightly underline interesting words or phrases in the original source.

3. Write the underlined words or phrases in the same order on a piece of scratch paper. Leave plenty of space between words and lines as you write so you can easily rearrange them or make adjustments and changes.

4. Study the words or phrases you have written on your scratch paper. Cut out anything that's dull or unnecessary. (The words from the original should be reduced by at least half.) Change the punctuation if you need to, but try not to add any words of your own.

5. Arrange and space the words, phrases, and lines on the page. Take the whole page into consideration as you shape your poem.

A. Play with line breaks.

> Lines may end at the end of a sentence.
> They may end at the end
> of a phrase
> or with a key
> word.

B. Arrange the words and sentences so they create a rhythm you like when you read the poem out loud.

C. Experiment with the white space.

1. You   can   space   words   apart   or   you   canrunthemtogether.

2. You can put key words

> on
> lines
> alone

D. Poems may have any shape you want.

```
=  =  =        = = = = = = = = =           = =              = = = =
=  =  =        = = = = = = = :       = = = = = = = = :      : = = = = = =
=  =  =        = = = = = = = =       = = = = = = = = = = =   : = = = = = =
=  =  =        = = =                 = = = = = = =           = = = =
=  =  =        = = = = = =           = = =                   = = = =
```

E. Words can be printed Large or small in color or in different **type** *faces*.

6. When the words, phrases, and lines are arranged just the way you want them, find a title, and add it to your poem.

7. At the bottom of the poem, tell where the words came from. Include the original author's name if possible. For example:

> —from "Blue Winds Dancing"
> by Thomas Whitecloud

Stories

We are told that students should be encouraged to write from personal experience. Trust your students to do this through fiction as well. They will write about the issues that are important to them. The following are useful story prompts:

1. The following may be used for individual students or as group prompts (in groups students pass their papers to the next student after completing each item):

   A. Write your name at the top of the page.
   B. Write a brief description of a setting for a story.
   C. Add and describe one character.
   D. Add and describe a second character.
   E. Describe a conflict between the two characters.
   F. Have one character make a statement in direct dialogue to develop the conflict.
   G. Let the second character respond.
   H. Describe the two characters engaged in some action.
   I. Write a brief dialogue between the characters.
   J. Bring the situation to a climax.
   K. Resolve the conflict. (For groups, return the sheet to the person whose name appears at the top of the page.)[23]

2. Directions for brainstorming (may also be used as a group activity):

   A. Write down three categories of people who might be in a group. For example: construction workers, kids on a sports team, or old people in a nursing home.
   B. Circle the group that most appeals to you .
   C. Create three characters in the circled group. Name and describe them.
   D. Choose one of the characters and write a brief description of something that happened to him or her in the past.
   E. Write a scene in which two of the three characters are talking about the third and something that happened recently to the third person. This dialogue should reveal what the two think about the third person and give clues to the personality and lives of the two speakers.
   F. Write a story based on the brainstormed material.[24]

3. Questions for creating a character:

   A. What is his or her name? Age? Height? Weight?
   B. What unusual characteristic does he or she have?
   C. What place does she or he have in the family? (Oldest, middle, or youngest child; parent?)
   D. Who is his or her best friend?
   E. Who is a rival or enemy?
   F. What is this person's favorite food?
   G. What is this person's most hated food?

H. What is this person's favorite activity?

I. Is he or she neat or untidy?

J. Does this person have a secret fear? If so, what is it?

K. Who are this person's heroes?

L. What is a major problem this character is facing?

M. What are some physical habits he or she has?

N. What is the most important thing that happened to this character in the past few months?

O. What would someone meeting this character for the first time notice first?

P. What is this character's biggest secret?

Q. Write a story or character sketch based on this material.[25]

The possibilities for student writing are limitless. As you plan, be sure your students write in a variety of formats for many audiences. You'll want them to write in quantity, but you need not grade and correct everything they do. Help your students see their progress as writers, and, most important, encourage them to evaluate their own writing to become independent and self-sufficient.

CHAPTER VI

Teaching Reading and Literature

- *Approaches to the Teaching of Literature*
- *Selecting Texts for Student Readers*
- *Planning for Readers' Responses*
- *Evaluating, Testing, Grading*

Teaching Reading and Literature

I love this book. It's scary though—it's about a cereal killer.

Many of us are teachers of English because of our love of literature. We may not remember becoming readers ourselves or recall a time when we didn't read for pleasure. We were the students who carried novels in our schoolbags to read at any opportunity. We read on the school bus, in the back of the classroom, on the porch in the summer, under the covers at night with a flashlight. We simply grew up loving to read. As teachers of literature, we share what we love best with our students, and we want them to respond as enthusiastically as we do. Frequently, however, our own students have told us they don't like to read, or they "sort of" like to read, or they used to read as children but they stopped when they got to high school. In frustration, we have tended to blame contemporary society, the changing family structure, or the influence and intrusion of the media for our students' attitudes. We have searched for ways to make our own teaching of reading and literature more effective. We not only want those students in our classrooms who enjoy reading to continue to be enthusiastic, but we also seek to make reading more enjoyable for those who read only dutifully, ploddingly, or not at all. In this chapter, we'll explore successful approaches to the teaching of literature, approaches that will help your students become active, enthusiastic readers.

APPROACHES TO THE TEACHING OF LITERATURE

Over the years, literature has been taught in a variety of ways, and we teachers have frequently emphasized one element in literature at the expense of others. For example, the historical approach emphasizes context, the biographical approach highlights the author and literary form. More recently we have focused on the "new criticism" which views the text as central to the process of literary analysis. Beginning in the late 1950s and continuing through the 1960s, this analytical approach was probably the most widely used, and many college English courses concentrated on such elements as literary structure, imagery, or symbolism and regarded each work as an entity isolated from history or society. Many of us took such courses as undergraduates and graduates, and when we became teachers, we tended to teach in the same way. Our high school classrooms became smaller versions of college classrooms as we lectured and our students took notes. If our students didn't respond to our requests for meaning, we often felt obliged to fill in the silences, and we gave students our answers.

Recent research in reading has begun to exert enormous influence in the way reading and literature are currently being taught at all academic levels and, in particular, in elementary and secondary classrooms. The *response-centered approach* emphasizes the reader as a key element in the creation of a literary work and suggests that we have placed too much stress on getting meaning from the literature alone and too little on seeing what skills our students bring to their reading. Louise Rosenblatt's transactional view of literature has been particularly influential in this regard. She views reading not as a passive activity in which the reader receives the meaning from the text but as an active, dynamic process by which the reader and the text interact to create the literary work. From this perspective, *how* a reader reacts to or engages with a text is as important as *what* the artist "intended" (or what we teachers believe is intended).[1] Rosenblatt also differentiates between *efferent reading* and *aesthetic reading*. Efferent reading relates to information to be acquired and is the kind of reading a student would do while reading a social studies text, for example. Aesthetic reading (reading literature) is different, and the focus, we are told, should be on what happens during the actual reading.

Does this mean that we should throw out the historical approach, the biographical approach, a focus on the text, for example? Of course not. Each is useful and appropriate at various times. However, as our concept of the reader has changed, we've learned to place a greater value on our students' responses to literature, and we allow literary evaluation to grow naturally from these responses. We also seek to move our students beyond naïve personal responses to responses which examine a text. We ask them to write and talk openly about their thoughts and feelings, to note and record important textual cues, and to make connections between literature and life. We promote analytical thinking and critical judgment without denying the pleasure of a personal response. The changes we are making in our own teaching, the enormous variety of responses we are designing for students, and our students' renewed enthusiasm for reading and literature reflect the impact of this influential research.

The Student's Role

We teach adolescents, young people emerging from the relatively untroubled world of childhood into adulthood. They arrive in our classrooms with enormous energy and endless contradictions. They know a little. They know a lot. They're innocent. They're sophisticated. They're happy. They're sad. They're filled with conflict. They're bored. They're exuberant. They're withdrawn. They challenge the authority they earlier accepted. They seek praise, yet they are highly critical of themselves and others. They want to be independent, yet they need to identify with a group. Their lives revolve around friendships and social relationships. In her highly influential book, *In the Middle,* Nancy Atwell points out that this "confusion, bravado, restlessness, preoccupation with peers, and the questioning of authority are not manifestations of poor attitude; they are hallmarks of this particular time of life."[2] This enormous energy of adolescence is exactly what we teachers must utilize in order to actively involve our students in their own learning.

The Teacher's Role

Because the best teaching of literature happens when teachers and students are involved in genuine dialogue and collaboration, your role as the teacher in the response-centered literature classroom is far different from the traditional role of lecturer at the front of the room. No longer will you do most of the talking and reading, nor will you be the final authority for every interpretation. Instead you will serve as a guide and resource who plans for and creates a learning environment that makes risk-taking possible and that fosters a wide variety of student responses.

1. Provide a literature-rich classroom and enable students to read.

A classroom that encourages students to become literate is one filled with books (fiction and nonfiction), short stories, biographies, autobiographies, poetry, magazines, newspapers, writings by students and teachers—all the materials real readers use. This is also a classroom that gives students choices concerning what it is they read, time for reading, and options for a variety of responses. Atwell has pointed out that what occurs in the everyday world is what should be happening in our classrooms. She suggests that those of us who grew up loving to read and who teach literature match the way we learned to read, the way we used our own reading process, against the way we teach it in our classrooms. For example, as readers we usually decided what it was we wanted to read. We read for pleasure and meaning, and we talked with others about what we read. We argued, exchanged bits of information, described what we liked or hated, and recommended books to others. We were captivated, and we found books we loved.[3] We can make this happen for our students as well.

Fill bulletin boards with reviews written by students and clipped from newspapers and magazines. Set aside a blackboard space or a large piece of paper as a graffiti board and encourage students to comment on their reading without giving away the plot (cryptic comments help motivate more reluctant readers). Students interview teachers and community members for a recommended reading list or produce a summer reading list based on recommendations by staff and students.

Should students really choose everything they read? Some teachers allow students to choose every text they read. This requires extensive resources and real administrative artistry on the part of the teacher. The best approach is to strike a balance between whole-class reading and individualized reading. You should make the selections for whole-class reading, choosing the best literature your students are capable of understanding reasonably well. (The choice of a common text depends, of course, on what is available to you in the book room or in a class anthology, what has preceded its study, and the needs, interests, and abilities of the students.)

Allow your students to pick their own texts for independent reading projects. Books for independent reading may be chosen from those on the shelves in your classroom or the school library. Often, students will bring books from home, and you can encourage them to trade with one another. Add a few books to your classroom collection each year. (Garage sales and Friends of the Library sales are good places to find inexpensive copies.) Over time you will also want to acquire smaller sets (five or six copies) of a variety of titles for students to read in smaller groups. By allowing for many choices, you will be able to respond to students from the broadest possible range of ability levels and backgrounds.

How can I justify giving secondary students reading time in class? I've got to cover a lot of material. If we expect our students to become readers, we have to ensure that reading happens. This involves blocks of time, and it may be our greatest gift to our students. The best approach is to build in and adjust time in connection with specific units. Some teachers work with individual students while the remainder of the class reads. Others feel reading time is so sacred that they allow no other activity to occur, and they model reading along with their students. Reading with your students will give you time to familiarize yourself with adolescent titles, including the ones students recommend to you. However you structure in-class reading time, it's important to remember that students need time—time to read and time to get "hooked" on reading.

I always have my students write about their reading. What's wrong with asking students to write a literary analysis after they've read? There's nothing wrong with this kind of response, but it shouldn't be the only response we expect from our students. In the past, we usually assigned writing at the end of a discussion or unit, and our purpose was to evaluate a student's understanding. Writing prior to reading or during reading can become a means of achieving understanding, a way to initiate inquiry or open a discussion. (Later in this chapter, we'll talk about a wide variety of writing activities for students throughout the reading process.)

2. Allow students to stop reading something they are not enjoying.

As readers, we sometimes begin a book, discover it isn't for us, and set it aside. Students should understand they also have this option in their independent reading.

3. Emphasize reading and literature as communication rather than as a series of subskills.

Offer complete pieces of literature to your students: stories, plays, novels, essays, poems. Excerpts from chapters, fragments, and isolated words, phrases or exercise paragraphs are useful in some contexts for mini-lessons. They should, however, never be used as a substitute for the literature itself.

4. Evaluate and monitor the pattern of classroom discussions and questions.

We need to analyze carefully the way our classroom discussions evolve. For example, do we encourage students to state and defend their opinions, or do we have a single interpretation in mind and lead the discussion in that direction? You'll want to foster a sense of exploration and discovery and work toward helping students go beyond "correct" answers or superficial responses to articulate, expand, and defend their own responses.

Questions have long been the staple of teachers' techniques for promoting comprehension. What's new is that we're learning to ask students to generate their own questions. The simplest approach at the beginning of a class period is to ask each student to write on a slip of paper a question or issue about his or her reading each considers important. You may ask students to read these aloud or collect the slips and choose one or several. The questions become the basis for a class discussion and can take most of one class period. You'll want to introduce this technique early in the year. At first, students' questions may resemble the discussion topics in a textbook, but over time your students will learn to depend on their own resources and their questions will become more insightful and sophisticated.

Discussion based on student-generated questions is an ideal small-group exercise. Each member of the group writes a list of questions about the text. The group sorts the questions and decides whether members will consider every question, only one question, or several. Following the group discussion, one member summarizes for the whole class while you or a designated student lists the major ideas on the blackboard.

In a response-centered classroom, teachers and students really listen to each other and authority is shared. Discussion revolves around students' feelings, questions, and responses and may result in a shared interpretation or several interpretations. There is as much student talk as teacher talk, and students are allowed to disagree with each other and with the teacher.[4] Keep the following suggestions in mind for effective discussions:

1. Allow time to elapse before responding to a student's comments. Encourage others to respond first and don't rush to fill up the silences.

2. Keep your responses neutral. Students are used to trying to guess what we want to hear, and comments such as "good point," or "I agree with you" perpetuate this kind of thinking.

3. Encourage each speaker to say more, to elaborate, to clarify or to explain: "Why?" "What do you mean?" "Tell us more," and "I don't understand" are the kinds of replies that foster discussion.

5. Provide students with a variety of ways to analyze and respond to a text.

There is no single approach or lesson plan which is appropriate for every piece of literature. A teacher must tailor assignments and activities to each text. Nevertheless, in doing so, we seek to provide a range of response types that allow students to back up their judgments: emotional, descriptive, autobiographical, interpretive, evaluative. We also encourage our students to respond in a variety of formats: essays, journals, discussion, creative writing, oral interpretation, visual responses. (Suggestions for these options are discussed later in this chapter.)

Does this mean my students should never read what scholars or critics have to say? Focusing on students' responses does not deny the importance of scholars and critics. Our students should test their responses against those of others. One approach is to distribute sample critiques after students have completed their own work and ask them to compare their responses to what critics have said about a text.

6. Plan for collaborative responses throughout the reading process.

Ideally, you will plan for a variety of responses from your students, both individually and in small and large groups. While solo exploration is a significant part of becoming a reader, small-group discussion is ideal for adolescents. Work in small groups ensures more student involvement. It also encourages students to communicate with one another in the kind of exploratory talk that allows them to take greater risks. The interaction that occurs in small groups helps students understand why they respond as they do, encourages them to develop responses independently of you, and motivates them to explore areas of agreement and disagreement with one another. Group work can occur at any time in the reading process: as a prereading activity, as an activity that occurs during reading to extend the understanding of the text, or as a culminating activity. (Suggestions for group activities are discussed in detail later in this chapter.)

7. Become involved in the student's entire reading process.

Rather than simply testing comprehension after the reading is completed, become involved in your students' entire reading process. Plan for student responses before, during, and after reading a text.

How about study guides? Won't these help students as they read? Generally, study guides aren't helpful. Most don't allow for sustained, extended responses to a text, and many require only "correct answers" or emphasize one specific skill. These often unrelated questions may actually fragment the reader's attention rather than help a student's understanding.[5] Although some formats can be excellent, most do little to enhance the reader's understanding or appreciation of a text.

When do I teach skills? Since you are involved in the students' entire process, and diagnosis and evaluation are ongoing activities, you will include mini-lessons whenever you see the need. You'll find advice on creating and teaching mini-lessons later in this chapter, along with samples you can adapt or use as presented.

8. Give students options and choices in responding to literature.

Provide many options and possibilities for responses and assignments. As with any skill, students need encouragement, practice, and experience in creating their own responses to what they have read. If you tell students early in the year, "Respond to this piece of literature," their reaction is likely to be puzzlement. However, after having plenty of experience with a variety of responses, most students will perceive a long list of options and their chief concern will be having to choose a single response from all the possibilities they envision.[6]

9. Plan for student self-assessment and evaluation.

Assessment happens any time in the reading process—as a prereading activity to discover what information students bring to the text, as a check for understanding during the reading process, or as a culminating activity. In addition, students learn assessment skills to evaluate their own responses and the responses of others. Your goal is to reduce the need for extensive teacher evaluation as students become involved in their own evaluation process. Ideally, you will spend more time working with students as they read and respond to their reading and less time making up tests and marking papers. (See Chapter 2 for a complete discussion of testing and grading.)

10. Encourage students to share their responses with a variety of audiences.

Plan for your students to respond to one another and to prepare presentations for other "real" audiences, such as adults outside the classroom. When students learn and practice a variety of responses and successfully present them to many audiences, they are more highly motivated to respond again.

SELECTING TEXTS FOR STUDENT READERS

Classroom Anthologies

Many literature anthologies contain excellent selections for young readers. The sequencing of materials can be helpful to a teacher as well. In too many cases, however, the literature found in these anthologies is excerpted from a larger text or is selected because it represents a "good" example of a literary device. Students may gain the false impression that many poets wrote only one poem or that a famous novel contains but one chapter. Some anthologies tend to promote knowledge about books and authors rather than fostering critical reading or a reader's personal response. In addition, the nature of the tasks that students are asked to perform in conjunction with the reading often does not reflect effective teaching practice. For example, questions at the end of the texts tend to perpetuate the reader's role as an essentially passive one and do little to encourage aesthetic reading. Too often, questions are based almost entirely on recall and comprehension and call for answers that can be located directly in the text. Such anthologies often do little to build on the student's background knowledge prior to reading a selection and offer few reading strategies for the reading process itself. Most anthologies omit activities aimed at promoting small-group discussion and creative dramatics and offer few suggestions for personal and imaginative writing. Too often the questions and suggested activities which follow the texts serve as an assessment of student comprehension rather than help students extend and elaborate on new learning. Questions tend to focus on isolated pieces of information that are likely to disrupt the reader's comprehension.[7]

Does this mean that you should abandon a classroom anthology? Not necessarily. If an anthology is all that is available to you, use it, but don't feel you must cover everything. Be selective in the assignments you make and examine the responses these materials call for. When the book selection committee meets or new texts are ordered, consider replacing or supplementing the anthology with whole-class sets of novels, poetry, drama, and nonfiction. If your goal is to develop the habit of personal reading in your students, you'll want to give them access to the real thing—books rather than textbooks.

Selection of Texts

As we choose literature texts for students in our classrooms, we need to keep in mind what it is we want our students to learn and what attitudes we want them to develop. We're convinced of the value of literature for our students. We believe it can stimulate their imagination, their intellect, and their emotions and provide vicarious experiences with new places, different times, and a wide variety of people. It can help them grow in knowledge and understanding as they ask themselves the fundamental questions people have asked through the ages. Nevertheless, what we teach is always a concern. Do we teach adolescent literature or do we teach the classics? Some educators feel that little of adolescent literature is as good as what has stood the test of time. They believe that if students are not exposed to the world's finest writing, many will never read it. In addition, curriculum guidelines and standardized tests often require the reading of some basic texts. On the other hand, we are told that we need to provide adolescents with literature that attracts them, satisfies their interests, and at the same time challenges them. Fortunately, the quantity and quality of literature written expressly for young adults has grown enormously in the past thirty years.

While we want our students to be exposed to the best our language and culture have to offer, most teachers arrive at a middle ground. Not every piece of adolescent literature is worthy of study. Not every classic is appropriate. Some texts are simply too difficult or too remote from our students' experience and may destroy their interest in reading and the possibility that they will ever read with enthusiasm. Using students' interests as a starting point, choose both classic and adolescent literature for your classroom. Select for whole-class study worthy pieces, both classic and contemporary, that clearly have something to say to today's young people; allow many options for your students' independent reading.

Helpful sources for selecting texts for the secondary classroom.

Your school librarian or media specialist is your single best guide as you select material for your classroom. He or she knows and has available a wide variety of selection tools and sources for recommended titles based on theme, interest, popularity, genre, and reading level. The following resources are also helpful for both you and your students as you make your selections:

Arbuthnot, May Hill. *Children and Books.* Boston: Scott Foresman, 1972. Intended primarily for elementary and junior high teachers, this book is considered a classic and includes extensive, annotated booklists and bibliographies.

Carrier, Warren and Kenneth Oliver, eds. *Guide to World Literature,* Urbana, Illinois: NCTE, 1980. This source is organized to help teachers approach world literature thematically, generically, historically. and comparatively.

McBride, William G., *High Interest—Easy Reading: A Booklist for Junior and Senior High School Students,* Urbana, Illinois: NCTE, 1990. This sixth edition contains nearly four hundred annotations in twenty-three categories.

Miller-Lachmann, Lyn, *Our Family, Our Friends, Our World: An Annotated Guide to Significant Multicultural Books for Children and Teenagers,* New Providence, New Jersey: R. R. Bowker, 1992.

Stensland, Anna Lee. *Literature by and About the American Indian,* Urbana, Illinois: NCTE, 1979.

Morris, Patricia S. and Margaret A. Berry, *Young Adult Reading Activities Library: Activities and Booklists for Grades 6–12,* West Nyack, New York: The Center for Applied Research in Education, 1993. This source has six volumes of annotated book lists divided by theme, with generic activity sheets for modern/realistic fiction, historical fiction, science fiction/fantasy, mystery and suspense, biography/autobiography, and nonfiction.

Wurth, Shirley, ed. *Books for You: A Booklist for Senior High Students,* Urbana, Illinois: NCTE, 1992. This source organizes and annotates fiction, nonfiction, poetry, and drama appropriate for adolescents in grades 9-12 by theme and genre.

English Journal offers numerous book- and- media- selection reviews in columns such as "Books for Young Adults," "Pick of the Paperback," and "Booksearch." The NCTE also publishes a useful bibliography, *Book and Non-Book Media* (1972), by Flossie L. Perkins, a guide to resources in many areas related to the teaching of English.

Although choosing a class novel usually depends on what is available in the bookroom, you may also wish to consult the following lists as you plan for collaborative and independent reading. These lists are intended to be a helpful starting point and are by no means inclusive.

"Classics" list.

Ray Bradbury, *Fahrenheit 451*

Dee Brown, *Bury My Heart at Wounded Knee*

Pearl S. Buck, *The Good Earth*

Lewis Carroll, *Alice's Adventures in Wonderland*

Willa Cather, *My Antonia*

Pat Conroy, *The Lords of Discipline*

Pat Conroy, *The Water is Wide*

Stephen Crane, *The Red Badge of Courage*

Alexander Dumas, Sr., *The Three Musketeers*

Alexander Dumas, Sr., *The Man in the Iron Mask*

F. Scott Fitzgerald, *The Great Gatsby*

William Golding, *Lord of the Flies*

Joanne Greenberg, *I Never Promised You a Rose Garden*

John Howard Griffin, *Black Like Me*

Judith Guest, *Ordinary People*

Nathaniel Hawthorne, *The House of Seven Gables*

Nathaniel Hawthorne, *The Scarlet Letter*

Ernest Hemingway, *For Whom the Bell Tolls*

Ken Kesey, *One Flew Over the Cuckoo's Nest*

John Knowles, *A Separate Peace*

Carson McCullers, *The Heart Is a Lonely Hunter*

Carson McCullers, *A Member of the Wedding*

Boris Pasternak, *Doctor Zhivago*

Alan Paton, *Cry, the Beloved Country*

Sylvia Plath, *The Bell Jar*

Erich Marie Remarque, *All Quiet on the Western Front*

Mary Shelley, *Frankenstein*

John Steinbeck, *The Grapes of Wrath*

Bram Stoker, *Dracula*

Harriet Beecher Stowe, *Uncle Tom's Cabin*

Jonathan Swift, *Gulliver's Travels*

Mark Twain, *The Adventures of Huckleberry Finn*

Mark Twain, *A Connecticut Yankee in King Arthur's Court*

Mark Twain, *The Prince and the Pauper*

Jules Verne, *Around the World in 80 Days*

Jules Verne, *Journey to the Center of the Earth*

Jules Verne, *20,000 Leagues Under the Sea*

Kurt Vonnegut, Jr., *Slaughterhouse Five*

Oscar Wilde, *The Picture of Dorian Gray*

Richard Wright, *Black Boy*

Richard Wright, *Native Son*

Mystery/detective.

Anything by the following authors: Lilian Jackson Braun, Agatha Christie, Mary Higgins Clark, Anna Clarke, Sir Arthur Conan Doyle, Dashiell Hammett, Tony Hillerman, P.D. James, Ngaio Marsh, or Dorothy Sayers.

Other suggested books:

Lois Duncan, *Down a Dark Hall*
Lois Duncan, *Killing Mr. Griffin*
Lois Duncan, *Stranger with My Face*
Lois Duncan, *Summer of Fear*
Elaine L. Konisburg, *Father's Arcane Daughter*
Madeleine L'Engle, *Arms of the Starfish*
Madeleine L'Engle, *Young Unicorns*
Cynthia Voigt, *Callender Papers*

Fantasy/science fiction.

Any books by Robert Heintein or Anne McCaffrey.

Douglas Adams, *The Hitchhiker's Guide to the Galaxy*
Douglas Adams, *Life, the Universe and Everything*
Douglas Adams, *The Restaurant at the End of the Universe*
Richard Adams, *Watership Down*
Peter Beagle, *Last Unicorn*
Ray Bradbury, *Fahrenheit 451*
Marion Zimmer Bradley, *The Mists of Avalon*
Arthur Clarke, *2001: A Space Odyssey*
Susan Cooper, *The Dark Is Rising*
Susan Cooper, *Greenwitch*
Susan Cooper, *Silver on the Tree*
Stephen R. Donaldson, *Illearth War*
Stephen R. Donaldson, *Lord Foul's Bane*
Ursula Le Guin, *Left Hand of Darkness*
Ursula Le Guin, *The Tombs of Atuan*
Ursula Le Guin, *The Wizard of Earthsea*
Robin McKinley, *Beauty*
Robin McKinley, *The Door in the Hedge*
Robin McKinley, *The Outlaws of Sherwood*
Mary Shelley, *Frankenstein*
Bram Stoker, *Dracula*
J.R.R. Tolkien, *The Hobbit*
J.R.R. Tolkien, *Lord of the Rings* trilogy
Terence H. White, *The Once and Future King*

Biography/autobiography.

Maya Angelou, *I Know Why the Caged Bird Sings*
Claude Brown, *Manchild in the Promised Land*
Alan Bullock, *Hitler: A Study in Tyranny*
Richard E. Byrd, *Alone*
Truman Capote, *In Cold Blood*
John Howard Griffin, *Black Like Me*
Alex Haley, *The Autobiography of Malcolm X*
Helen Keller, *The Story of My Life*
Mary MacCracken, *Circle of Children*
Mary MacCracken, *Lovey: A Very Special Child*
Robert Massie, *Nicholas and Alexandra*
Nancy Milford, *Zelda: A Biography*
John C. Neihardt, *Black Elk Speaks*
Roger Shattuck, *Forbidden Experiment: The Story of the Wild Boy of Aveyron*
Evans G. Valens, *The Other Side of the Mountain*
Booker T. Washington, *Up From Slavery*
Donald Woods, *Biko*
Richard Wright, *Black Boy*

Historical fiction.

Jean Auel, *Clan of the Cave Bear*
Jean Auel, *Valley of the Horses*
Thomas Berger, *Little Big Man*
Joan Blos, *A Gathering of Days*
Hal Borland, *When the Legends Die*
Carol Brink, *Caddie Woodlawn*
Dee Brown, *Bury My Heart at Wounded Knee*
Pearl S. Buck, *The Good Earth*
Walter Clark, *The Ox-Bow Incident*
Howard Fast, *April Morning*
Esther Forbes, *Johnny Tremain*
Paula Fox, *Slave Dancer*
Ernest Gaines, *The Autobiography of Miss Jane Pittman*
Bette Greene, *Summer of My German Soldier*
Irene Hunt, *Across Five Aprils*
Irene Hunt, *Up a Road Slowly*
Oliver La Farge, *Laughing Boy*
Margaret Mitchell, *Gone with the Wind*
Scott O'Dell, *Sarah Bishop*

Scott O'Dell, *Sing Down the Moon*

Erich Marie Remarque, *All Quiet on the Western Front*

Mary Renault, *The Bull from the Sea*

Mary Renault, *The King Must Die*

Conrad Richter, *A Light in the Forest*

Elizabeth George Speare, *Bronze Bow*

Mary Stewart, *The Crystal Cave*

Irving Stone, *The Agony and the Ecstasy*

Mildred Taylor, *Roll of Thunder, Hear My Cry*

Historical fiction: Twentieth-Century Wars.

James Clavell, *King Rat*

Joseph Heller, *Catch 22*

Ernest Hemingway, *Farewell to Arms*

Ernest Hemingway, *For Whom the Bell Tolls*

James Michener, *Bridges at Toko-Ri*

Erich Marie Remarque, *All Quiet on the Western Front*

Nevil Shute, *A Town Like Alice*

Dalton Trumbo, *Johnny Got His Gun*

Leon Uris, *Exodus*

Herman Wouk, *The Caine Mutiny*

Herman Wouk, *War and Remembrance*

Herman Wouk, *Winds of War*

At least part of your curriculum should be devoted to texts selected by students. Some will want to read books about characters like themselves facing similar problems. Many will choose escape books for pleasure reading: romances such as Silhouette and Harlequin; suspense stories such as Tom Clancy's *The Hunt for Red October*; gothic stories by Stephen King or V.C. Andrews; and science fiction and fantasy with titles such as *Sundrinker, Godslayer,* and *Trekmaster.* Personal standard of choice will be modified as readers develop and mature. Their judgment will be sharpened through classwork, the reading of reviews, and discussions with classmates. The following is a sample list of high-interest, easy-reading books for even the most reluctant reader in your classroom:

Robert Cormier, *After the First Death*

Robert Cormier, *The Cholocate War*

Lois Duncan, *They Never Came Home*

S.E. Hinton, *The Outsiders*

S.E. Hinton, *That Was Then, This Is Now*

S.E. Hinton, *Tex*

Irene Hunt, *The Lottery Rose*

Irene Hunt, *No Promises in the Wind*

Ron Jones, *The Acorn People*

James Vance Marshall, *A River Ran Out of Eden*

James Vance Marshall, *Walkabout*

Harry Maser, *Snowbound*

Scott O'Dell, *Sing Down the Moon*

Gary Paulsen, *Dancing Carl*

Gary Paulsen, *Dog Song*

Gary Paulsen, *Hatchet*

Gary Paulsen, *Sentries*

Gary Paulsen, *Tracker*

Katherine Peterson, *Jacob Have I Loved*

Jack Schafer, *Shane*

Elizabeth George Speare, *The Sign of the Beaver*

Glendon Swarthout, *Bless the Beasts and Children*

Theodore Taylor, *The Cay*

Lawrence Yep, *Liar, Liar*

Censorship

Some books are perhaps not appropriate for secondary students. Whether we call it selection or censorship, it is a dilemma faced by every concerned English teacher. Inevitably, if you are teaching literature, some of the works you use will be objectionable to someone either because of the subject matter or the style in which they are written. Consider books carefully before adding them to your lists of recommended reading. It's important that you be familiar with the titles on your list. It's never a good idea to use someone else's list, because what might be acceptable in one community may not be in another. The best way to become familiar with adolescent literature is to read it. After all, no list can take the place of an enthusiastic teacher recommending a title. Your most helpful source in this regard is your school librarian who is usually an avid reader able to recommend appropriate novels for students.

In most classrooms, the practice of forcing students to read something that they or their parents find objectional can be solved by providing students with options. Most parents who find fault with a particular selection are satisfied if they are told that students can read alternative texts. Complaints can be handled individually so that no books will be censored for the whole class. It is less important that all students read a particular book, than that they read and respond to something. Before ordering classroom sets for required reading, carefully consider your rationale for doing so. In addition, your English department should encourage a carefully written rationale for each required text. The following questions provide a good model for book selection.[8]

1. For what age group is this book appropriate?

2. To what objectives does this book lend itself?

3. In what ways will this book meet these objectives?

4. What problems of style, tone, or theme or possible grounds for censorship exist in this book?

5. How will you meet these problems?

6. Assuming that these objectives are met, how will students be different because of the reading of this book?

7. What are other appropriate books a student might read in place of this book?

8. What reputable sources have recommended this book? What have critics said of it?

In addition, be sure you know whether your department or school district has a policy for dealing with challenged resources. If community members propose to ban a book in question for an entire class or from the school library, it's important that you have a school policy for dealing with this ahead of time.

Setting Up a Sequence for Teaching

You have from 32 to 36 or more weeks divided into semesters, trimesters, or quarters and from four to eight marking periods in the school year. What will be your plan? Although it is tempting to just follow an anthology from cover to cover, you'll want to resist this approach. You'll begin by addressing some basic concerns: What are your goals? What texts are available to you? What are your students' interests and abilities? What response activities will you include?

Planning is essential, but don't make your design so rigid that there is little room for student input or fascinating detours. Begin by deciding on some kind of organizational framework for each unit. Typical frameworks include the following:

Literary types—a unit may be based on a particular literary classification:

- Nonfiction: essays, biography, autobiography.
- Fiction: novels, novellas, short stories, poetry, drama.

Fiction units may also be designed according to specific categories within the genre: mystery stories, science fiction, detective stories, multicultural literature, westerns, comedy, or tragedy, for example. In structuring a unit in this way, it is important that the focus be on the literature and not exclusively on the characteristics of the genre. A teacher planning a unit that involves reading several novels might use the earlier lists as a starting point. For example:

1. The whole class reads and responds to a novel from the "classics" list.

2. Next, groups of students choose a title from the biography/autobiography list or the historical novel list.

3. Finally, students choose independent reading titles from the mystery/detective list or the fantasy/science fiction list.

Historical survey—American and British literature have often been taught as survey courses in which texts are approached chronologically. This ordering is becoming less and less common in secondary schools because it tends to emphasize knowledge about books and authors without helping students develop an appreciation of the literature itself.

Individual authors—Units structured around a number of works by the same author can help more able students gain insight into an author. This is not as satisfactory an approach for less able students.

Thematic units—Grouping literature by subject or theme is one of the most common and popular organizational frameworks designed by English teachers. Some popular themes include: growing up, heroes and heroines, survival, death and dying, family relationships, love, alienation, justice, and war. (The selection tools mentioned earlier in this chapter offer additional themes.) A thematic structure is especially effective because you can appeal to your students' interests and at the same time involve them in a wide variety of texts and genres. However, one danger in creating thematic units is that students may encounter the same themes over and over. You'll want to consult with your colleagues at each grade level to avoid this possibility.

Suppose you or you and the class have chosen the theme "growing up." You might begin, for example, by picking a single novel for the entire class. In this case it could be *Great Expectations* or *To Kill a Mockingbird*. By having chosen a theme, you have also limited the scope of student responses. In other words, you won't try to include everything there is to be said about this novel. In *To Kill a Mockingbird* your focus will be on Scout's growing up and what she learns and comes to know as she matures. Other insights will emerge as the class responds to the text—and you will welcome them—but these will not be paramount. Next, you or you and your students will select five or six related texts. For example:

- Short stories
  —John Updike, "A & P" and James Joyce, "Araby"

- Poetry
  —Janice Ian, "At Seventeen" and William Stafford, "Fifteen"

- Drama
  —William Shakespeare, *Romeo and Juliet* and Carson McCullers, *The Member of the Wedding*

- Film
  —*The Chocolate War* (based on Robert Cormier's novel)

You might expect every student to read one of each of these options or you might assign students to small groups on the basis of the one text they want to read. Finally, plan for students to independently read self-selected texts with a similar theme.

Many variations on this framework are possible, and you'll want to experiment with several. Small-group activities can be used as a starting point from which to individualize whole-class activities. For example:

1. Each group picks a particular author. The members of a group read the same book by their author and collaborate in a group response.
2. Next, individuals choose an additional text by the same author for independent study.
3. Finally, the whole class collaborates in producing a group response: an annotated reading list for students in another classroom, or a display piece, for example.

A good organizational framework and sequence will allow you to keep the entire class together part of the time. It will also provide opportunities for students to work together in smaller groups, and it will include student-selected independent reading options. In this classroom, you will serve as a guide and resource person. You'll determine when students read, write, speak, and listen. You'll organize the class into groups for reading or discussion or response projects, and you'll bring them back together for whole-class projects. You'll provide additional material in mini-lessons when it is significant. You'll call attention to certain parts of a work and provide background information that can help the text come alive. You'll guide some of the talk and provide a wide variety of options for student response. This kind of teaching is exhilarating. When we discard the certainty of lectures, we won't necessarily control all the outcomes. We will, however, create a classroom in which we and our students learn from one another.

PLANNING FOR READERS' RESPONSES

Responses occur at any time in the reading process: before reading (to build on prior knowledge), during reading (to develop a reader's expertise), and following reading (to share some understanding of a text). You will also want your students to respond in a variety of ways. Our goal as teachers has always been to integrate the language arts—reading, writing, speaking, and listening. When you plan for many response options, a true integration of these elements in your classroom is possible. The following is a sampling of responses you can adapt for students in your classroom:

Responses *Before* Reading

1. Take time at the beginning of a class period to talk informally about anything you are reading, and encourage your students to do the same. (You might have students do this in small groups as well.) At some point have each student talk about one text he or she would enthusiastically recommend to other class members. Also consider using *The Open Door: When Writers First Learned to Read* (Steven Gilbar, ed., Boston: David R. Godine, 1989). This is a treasury of recollections about reading experiences of famous authors.

2. Provide appropriate texts for students whose reading skills are limited. Consult your school's reading specialist and librarian for help in obtaining such texts, and invite them into your classroom to talk with students about their recommendations. A list of titles of recommended books for reluctant young adult readers is also available in a brochure from the Library Association Graphic Department. For one free copy, send a self-addressed, stamped business-size envelope to YALSA Office, 50 East Hurson Street, Chicago, Illinois 60611.

3. Invite other teachers and community members into your classroom to speak about the importance of reading in their lives. (Videotape these speakers for future classes.)

4. Read a few lines or a few paragraphs from some popular selections to whet students' appetites. For example, the first line, "They murdered him," from Robert Cormier's *The Chocolate War* is sure to hook many readers.

5. Read several paragraphs or pages of a selected text to students before they begin reading it themselves. Ask them to speculate about what will happen next or what kind of a person a character will be.

6. Don't stop reading aloud to students when they reach high school. The following short stories are highly recommended by classroom teachers:

Robert Block, "The Hell-Bound Train"

Kate Chopin, "The Story of an Hour"

Mona Gardner, "The Dinner Party"

Charlotte Perkins Gilman, "The Yellow Wallpaper"

Zenna Henderson, "The Believing Child"

Langston Hughes, "Thank You, Ma'am"

Richard Matheson, "Born of Man and Woman"

Guy de Maupassant, "Old Mother Savage"

Octavio Paz, "The Blue Bouquet"

Quentin Reynold, "A Secret for Two"

J.D. Salinger, "The Laughing Man"

John Updike, "A & P"

Donald Vining, "The Old Dog"

Kurt Vonnegut, "EPICAC"

7. Pose a whole-class or small-group discussion question related to a story before the class has read it: "What would you do if someone had borrowed some expensive piece of jewelry to wear to a party and lost it?" (Guy de Maupassant's "The Necklace"); "Suppose a battered fence separates your house from your neighbor's. Should your father pay a hundred dollars to have it repaired or should he tear it down to give the neighborhood children room to play?" (Robert Frost's "Mending Wall") ; "Can there be heroes in an impersonal, technological society?" (Arthur Miller's *Death of a Salesman* or Robert Cormier's *"I am the Cheese"*) .

8. Read a story or several poems to students prior to their reading similar material. Show what good oral reading is and how it recreates a storyteller's voice. Call on parents, talented students, members of local amateur or professional drama groups, storytellers, or community writers reading from their own work to demonstrate oral reading. Play recordings of authors and professional readers. Ask students in your classroom to prepare their own selections for oral reading either as a beginning or a culminating activity. Good sources for storytellers include: Bob Barton's *Tell Me Another: Storytelling and Reading Aloud at Home, at School, and in the Community* (Portsmouth, New Hampshire: Heinemann, 1986) and Caroline Feller Bauer's *Handbook for Storytellers* (Chicago: American Library, 1977).

9. Use a film or recorded literature to begin a unit.

10. Ask students to role play a situation similar to one they will encounter in a text. For example, before reading *The Diary of a Young Girl* organize small groups and instruct each that they must sit together but make no noise for a designated period of time. They are not to speak aloud nor do anything that will make even the slightest noise. Warn them that any noise might mean discovery and death. Finally, have students write about their feelings and describe the effect of the silence upon other members of their group. Meet in small or large groups to discuss and share observations before beginning to read.[10]

11. Display picture books and art books reflecting ideas or a setting related to the literature to be read.

12. In preparation for reading, students:

    a. write about the unit theme or topic at the beginning of a unit. (Students might be asked to write about the Holocaust before reading Elie Wiesel's *Night,* for example.) This will help you determine what students already know, think, or feel about a topic.

    b. write in the same genre as the one to be read. For example, students write poetry before reading it, write dialogue before reading drama, or write a description of a special place before reading Maya Angelou's description of Stamps, Arkansas, in *I Know Why the Caged Bird Sings.* Writing in this manner helps students develop a strong sense of a genre's features as well as its possible variations.[11] The comparisons are not meant to suggest that the author's version is better than the student's, but they help students appreciate the talent and craft of a successful writer.

    c. research information either individually or in teams prior to reading a historical novel or older work. Students might research the Roaring Twenties before reading *The Great Gatsby,* for example.

    d. write about the same problem as that posed in a piece of literature:

        —"You have just been marooned on a desert island that has vegetable and animal life and fresh water. Discuss what you must do to ensure your survival."(*Lord of the Flies*)

        —"List the names of some people and circumstances that irritate you. Then write a description of these irritating people or circumstances." ("The Telltale Heart")

        —"Write about an event or experience in your life that has caused you to grow up a bit. Explain its impact on you. How did it effect your thinking?" (*To Kill a Mockingbird*)

    e. design a rating scale or a chart: "Make a list of the characteristics of an effective leader. Rank them." (*Lord of the Flies*)

Responses *During* Reading

1. Plan discussions based on a wide variety of open-ended questions, questions generated by the students themselves about meaning, intent, and ideas.

2. Review an important passage in a text, and then pose a specific question. Students write their answers before an oral discussion so that each can formulate an opinion.

3. Read to students but stop several times for written responses:

How does this passage make you feel?

What details stand out? Why?

Does this passage remind you of an experience you have had?

What might happen next? How might the story end?

What questions do you have about the characters? the action? the setting?

4. Suggest that students draw a map to accompany a text. For example, have students consult the text to draw a map of the neighborhood in *To Kill a Mockingbird* or sketch the layout of the living quarters in *Diary of a Young Girl*. Still another option is to have students draw a map tracing the route characters follow in any story which involves a journey (*Huckleberry Finn,* for example). The NCTE catalogue lists a variety of historical literary maps that are useful as models.

5. Either individually or collaboratively rewrite parts of a novel as a play or radio or television script. Videotape the scene for a class presentation or deliver it "live" before the class.

6. Rewrite a portion of the text from a new point of view. Students might, for example, assume the role of Lady Macbeth's doctor and write the doctor's version of her sleepwalking scene. The following is a sample assignment for *To Kill a Mockingbird* that helps readers sort and organize information in preparation for experimenting with point of view. Students may work independently or in groups.

The Rest of the Story

A. Scout is the narrator of this story. On Halloween night she and Jem walk from the schoolhouse to their home, "their longest journey together." Because Scout is unable to remove her ham costume, Jem leads her. She can only tell us what she hears, smells, and feels. Examine the text carefully and make a list of everything that happens from the time Scout leaves the schoolhouse until she finally removes her costume and sees someone carry Jem into the house.

B. Boo Radley is also on the path that night. "Get into his skin" and write several paragraphs from his point of view telling us what he knows about what happened on the path that night.

Another approach is to assign students to groups and have each respond to a single event from a different character's point of view. For example, Atticus, Sheriff Tate, Mr. Cunningham, Dill, Tom, or Mr. Underhill might each recall the mob scene in front of the jail.

7. Ask students to respond to a text by adopting a newspaper format and recasting information as a news story based on the following questions.

Who was involved?
What happened?
When did it happen?
Where did it happen?
Why did it happen?

"Interview" the characters involved and quote them in the article. A news report could be written for a battle in *Red Badge of Courage* or the trial in *To Kill A Mockingbird*. Students might create an underground flier designed to stir up a revolution against MacBeth. "Dear Abby" letters and responses are also useful formats. Aunt Alexandria might seek advice on how to handle Scout, or Scout might ask for help in getting along with the teenaged Jem. Since Mr. Webb (*Our Town*) is the editor of the newspaper, he will write his daughter's obituary. Students might write it for him. A description of George and Emily's wedding for the society page or a feature article on George's high school career in baseball for the sports page are equally good responses.

8. In dealing with a text that uses flashback, have students rearrange the events and list them in strict chronological order. Finally, discuss what was probably the author's reason for altering the sequence and what the story lost or gained as a result.[12]

9. In dealing with a longer text, such as a novel, set target dates for reading. Plan an activity for an agreed upon set of pages, but caution those who have read ahead not to spoil the pleasure of others by discussing beyond that point. A "jigsaw" is a useful group activity for students working with longer texts. All students read the assigned material but each group is responsible for discussing a portion of the material. Final reports complete the jigsaw and cover all the material. To create a group jigsaw for several chapters of a novel, assign a specific number of pages to each group. Ask each to discuss its material by pointing out significant events or passages and relating these to ideas and themes generated by earlier class assignments. Finally, call on each group to summarize its discussion for the entire class.

Jigsaws can be used in a variety of ways. In discussing characterization, for example, assign a different major character to each group. Ask each to decide upon three adjectives that best describe the character and to explain the reasons for selecting them. Each group finds a passage or several passages in the text that best reveal the character's personality. Groups report to the class as a whole. Conclude with a whole-class discussion of the author's handling of characterization.

Individual Responses *during* reading.

Too often we have had students write about literature only after they have finished reading. An alternative which allows students to respond to the text as they read is the *reading journal* or *log*. This approach is especially desirable because writing during reading encourages students to consider the kinds of questions that take readers further in understanding than they might go on their own. It helps them gather information, reflect upon it, and make connections between what they are learning and their own lives. They:

- make note of interesting points or passages or anything they want to remember to talk about later;
- jot down questions as they read;
- make predictions about what will happen next;
- elaborate on a text by pretending;
- summarize ideas;
- evaluate any classroom activities; and
- respond to prompts supplied by the teacher.

A notebook for the reading journal serves to keep the entries together and organized. (Invite students to design covers for the journal which reflect themselves or the class.) The teacher reads the entries quickly and responds to provocative ideas and observations. Correctness and editing problems are not noted because the journal is intended to be a risk-free setting for experimenting with and exploring language and ideas.

Journals are also an effective evaluative tool. They will help you know your students better: why they choose particular books, why they favor some authors, and who or what influences them in the selection of texts. They will also help you check on student progress and the effectiveness of classroom activities, resources, readings and discussions. They can help you know when to present information, when to present it differently, or when to reteach a particular concept. Asking students to read excerpts from their journals is an excellent way to initiate a discussion. Ideas and observations generated in the journal may also serve as preliminary work for a more formal response following the reading. Finally, journals encourage students to think and write about literature without the constraints of the book report form, which seldom allows students to write about their own feelings and often serves as a test of reading without fostering a love for it. The following questions may be suggested to students who are writing in journals . They can also be used as prompts for whole-class or small-group discussions if you do not plan to have students write in a journal.

1. What kind of a person is _____? What is your evidence?

2. If _____ were living today, what kind of clothes would he or she wear?

3. Are _____'s actions surprising to you? Can they be accounted for in the story?

4. Suppose _____ were in a (hypothetical situation). What would he or she do? How does this differ from what you would do?

5. What do other characters say about _____? Why do they feel this way?

6. How does _____ treat other characters in the story? What evidence do you have?

7. How and why does _____ change in the course of the story?

8. Why do _____ and _____ relate to one another the way they do?

9. How do the other characters respond to _____ in the story? Why is this so?

10. Who are the "good" people in this text? What makes them "good"? (Who are the "bad" . . .?)

11. What is one problem in the story? Which character has this problem and how is he or she trying to solve it? Would you approach the problem the same way?

12. Who is the narrator of the story you are reading? Why do you think the author chose this narrator?

13. Finish this sentence: "I love the way the author . . ."

14. Have you read any other books by the author you're reading now? If so, how does this one compare? If not, would you like to?

15. Write a brief interview with the main character of your book.

16. Write a letter to me about the kind of story you like best. Why do you like this?

17. How did the author of your book get you interested in the story?

18. Write me a letter telling me about the setting of the story you are reading. Why do you think the author chose this time and place?

19. What do you think will happen next? What evidence did you use from what you've already read to help you make your prediction?

As valuable as journals are, managing them can become a real concern. You'll want to avoid lugging around boxes or spending hours and hours reading. One solution is to limit journal writing to your students' independent reading projects. As students use class time to read, pick up several journals each day, read them, write comments and hand them back. This running commentary might constitute the entire "study" of an independent reading project. Form 6.1, "Directions for a Reading Journal," can be distributed to students when you make the assignment. Reading journals are most effective at the secondary level if the assignment is fairly structured. This is especially true for students who are keeping a reading journal for the first time if you want them to record their reactions on more than a superficial level. A grade may be awarded according to how many of the suggested entries a student attempts (14 – 17 = A, 11 – 13 = B, 8 – 10 = C, for example). Form. 6.2, "Reading Journal Self-Evaluation" encourages students to become a part of the evaluation process.

6.1   Directions for a Reading Journal

A reading journal is not the same as a writing journal. Your entries are to be responses to the literature you are reading. Write often, using the following suggestions as a guide. Use as many of these suggestions as possible. Think independently and write imaginatively. Your ideas, opinions, and thoughts about your reading are important. Your journal grade will be based on the quality of your entries as well as the variety and number of responses you write.

1. Explain how you chose your book.

2. Write about a memory or experience of your own that is similar to something you've read in your book.

3. Make as long a list as possible of questions that arise as you read.

4. Write a reaction to something you have read.

5. Write a brief summary of several pages or a chapter. Do not, however, write a summary each time you write.

6. Become one of the characters in your book and write a letter or poem from that character's point of view.

7. Write an interview between you and the main character of your book.

8. Illustrate a scene or draw a map or symbol that reflects your book.

9. Comment on the author's technique: choice of words or the way he or she tells a story. Do you admire the way the author writes? Why or why not?

10. Before you have finished your book, make a prediction about how you think it will end. What makes you think it will end this way?

11. Do you think the title of this book is a good one? Why or why not? What are some other possible titles?

12. Imagine you are one of the characters in the story. Write a diary entry that reflects your thoughts and feelings about an event in your life.

13. Discuss a memorable scene from your book.

14. Write a letter to the author beginning, "I have just finished reading your novel, and I'd like you to know that . . ."

15. Find and read a review of the book you are reading and discuss your reaction to it.

16. Who else should read this book? Why? Who shouldn't read it? Why?

17. What book do you plan to read next? Explain.

Name _____ Date _____

6.2 Reading Journal Self-Evaluation

1. How many entries have you made in your reading journal since you began? _____

2. Do you write a response nearly every time you read? _____ Explain. _____
   _____

3. On an attached sheet, copy an entry which is fairly typical of the type of entries you write.

4. On an attached sheet, copy an entry you consider to be one of your best. Explain why you chose it. _____
   _____
   _____

5. Write a short analysis of your reading journal. Will you make any changes in your next entries, for example, or are you satisfied with your approach to journal writing?
   _____
   _____
   _____
   _____
   _____
   _____

6. How do you feel about keeping a reading journal? Is this assignment helpful to you as you read and respond to literature? Please explain. _____
   _____
   _____
   _____
   _____
   _____
   _____

Individual or Group Responses after Reading

Traditionally, many of us have asked students to write a critical analysis following their reading of a piece of literature. This is perfectly acceptable. There are, however, many other options you should consider as culminating activities. These options appeal to students with a variety of learning styles. They will use their higher order thinking skills as they recast their responses in new and delightful ways.

1. Assemble a collection of quotable quotes from the text. Groups could bind these in a booklet for a class display.

2. Illustrate a series of memorable scenes to display on a bulletin board, to present to the class on an overhead projector, or to bind in a booklet.

3. Create a calendar to supplement a literary work. The top third will include an appropriate illustration with a written explanation. Below, indicate the month and days and note important dates based on the text.

4. Design a time line to fit the story. Include all the main events.

5. Create a diorama or shadow box—a three-dimensional representation of a significant scene or scenes presented in a confined space such as a shoe box.

6. Act as a literary critic or review board and prepare a review of the book to share with the class.

7. Become one of the characters in the text and write and deliver a monologue for that character, using props and costumes. Groups should include several characters and perhaps add the author and a critic.

8. Write and deliver an interview of several characters in a story. Videotape or tape record the interview to present to the class, or deliver it "live."

9. Write a poem about each character in the book. Collect all of the poems in a class booklet. The poems might have an additional unifying format such as structure—acrostic, for example. Another option for creating a poem is to ask each student to write a paragraph about a character and convert it to free verse with an emphasis on economy, white space, and line breaks. Students might also create "found" poems about a literary character based on significant lines and passages in the text itself.

10. Write a poem based on the mood, images, or feelings aroused by a story.

11. Stage an author's day. Each student shares his or her own writing either orally or in some published form.

12. Write an exchange of letters between characters or authors from the same text or separate texts.

13. Compare a book's, film's, and television program's handling of the same story. How does the story change with each medium and why?

14. Suppose the author of the book you've read is a friend of yours. Write an imaginary telephone conversation between the two of you in which you discuss the book you've read.

15. Create puppets (paper bags or socks, for example) and dramatize a scene from a piece of literature.

16. Write a TV or radio script for one of the stories you have read. Students either

turn their script in to the teacher or assemble a cast and videotape it or perform it for an audience.

17. Construct objects which reflect items in the literature: shields, flags, or reproductions, for example. This might involve research as well as keeping a journal or log to document the formulation of ideas, the acquisition of materials, and a description of the object and its connection to the piece of literature. Students use their speaking skills as they present and explain their objects to the class.

18. Write a short book review, and deliver it in the school's morning announcements.

19. Interview classmates and teachers. Annotate and post a recommended reading list for next year's students.

20. Write telephone-answering-machine messages or bumper stickers for several characters in a selection.[13]

21. After reading a required text, write a letter to the district's director of curriculum recommending for or against the novel's selection.

22. Make a list of all an author had to know in order to write a particular story.

23. After reading a book about war, interview people of various ages who have served in wars. Report these findings in writing or in a panel discussion.

24. Research the life of the author, then write a script for an interview.

25. Write an autobiography for one of the characters in the text. The autobiography could span the years from childhood to the time the reader first meets the character in the text. Students brainstorm a list of make-believe interview questions and use the invented answers as the basis for the autobiography. For example:

    In what kind of family did you grow up?
    How did you and your parents get along?
    What responsibilities did you have growing up?
    What were the latest fads when you were a teenager?
    What concerned you most when you were a teenager?
    What is your most vivid childhood memory?

26. Create a crossword puzzle using information from the text.

27. Write a song—music and lyrics that reflect the text—and perform it for the class.

28. Choose one character in the text. Bring an object from home (don't purchase anything new) that you might give this character as a gift. Explain to the class why the gift would be appropriate.

29. Write a letter of recommendation for a job for a character in a literary work.

30. Decide what is the best book you've ever read. Write a letter to someone who doesn't like to read, convincing him or her to read your book.

31. Hold a reading fair. Include displays: posters, original student writing, art reproductions, illustrations, collages, mobiles, book covers, models. Include taped music and perform scenes from literature, invite parents and friends, or take the entire production to a class of younger students.

The sample assignments, 6.3, "A Booksellers' Day," 6.4, "Independent or Group Response Projects for a Novel," 6.5, "A Novel Response," and 6.6, "Responding to a Book," are excellent options to consider as you plan response projects for your classroom.

© 1994 by The Center for Applied Research in Education

Name_____ Date _____

6.3   A Booksellers' Day

Your assignment has been to read a book independently. You were asked to select your own book, choosing one that is worthwhile and truly enjoyable. After you have completed your independent reading, we will hold a classroom booksellers' day on _____. Each of you will try to "sell" your book in a book talk. Plan to use visual aids to accompany your "pitch," as well as props, costumes, and/ or music. Visual aids might include:

- advertising posters
- a book jacket of your own design
- advertising fliers to distribute to the class (I'll help you make copies.)
- bumper stickers
- lapel buttons
- bookmarks
- business cards
- a magazine spread
- transparencies for the overhead projector (I'll show you how to make these.)
- your own videotaped advertisement
- an ordinary object that represents the book in some way.

The following is the suggested format for your talk:

1. Set up your props and materials.

2. Introduce the book. Show it to your audience. Be sure to give the title and author. Write the title and the author on the board or refer to it in one of your visual aids.

3. You may want to provide some background about the author. This should be only a brief portion of your presentation. Be sure to tell your audience what source you have used for this information.

4. Briefly summarize the book. Spend no more than a minute or two on this portion of your talk. (Decide whether you should reveal the ending.)

5. Read a brief excerpt from the book. The passage you select should be a significant passage that describes a main character in some way, represents an important point in the plot, or reflects the author's style.

6. Review the book. This is the important part of your talk. You might comment on the book's theme, problem, conflict, character development, or believability . Your opinion counts. What did you like? What might other readers like? Relate your talk to the visual material included in your presentation. Make a recommendation to other students. "Sell" this book to those you believe would enjoy it.

7. If the book has been made into a movie and you have seen it, you might also want to compare and contrast the book and the film. If you wish, you can bring in the video and show a short clip (no more than two minutes). This could count as a visual aid. If you plan to do this, make arrangements with me ahead of time to have a video player and monitor in the room.

The following scoring sheet will be used in evaluating your presentation:

1. Visual aids   10 points

2. Props or costume or music   10 points

3. Introduction and conclusion   5 points

4. Info. about the author   5 points

5. Brief plot summary   5 points

6. Excerpt from the book   5 points

7. Review and "selling" of book   <u>10 points</u>

   Total   50 points

6.4   Independent or Group Response Projects for a Novel

We have come to understand that there are many ways we can respond to literature. After you have finished your novel, choose one of the suggested projects. You may complete this assignment independently or you may organize a group and work cooperatively. Presentations are scheduled for _____. Choose one of the following options:

1. Design a time line to fit the story. Use illustrations and include all the main events.

2. Draw several cartoon strips showing the main parts of the story. What happened in the beginning, the middle, the end?

3. Plan a filmstrip with 15 to 25 frames to retell the story with pictures and text. The frames should recount the story in sequence. The first frames will be the title and credits. The last frame will be "The End."

4. Create and produce an alphabet book. Show knowledge of characters and events through the letters of the alphabet.

5. Write a poem about each major character in the book. Collect all poems in a bound book. Include illustrations.

6. Make a "wanted" poster for a character in the book. Include a drawing, physical description, a list of the character's misdeeds, the reward being offered, and any other important information.

7. Write and deliver a monologue for one or more characters. Use props and costumes for the presentation.

8. Prepare a newspaper account of a major event in the book. If a group works on this project, produce a complete issue.

9. Prepare a short presentation to introduce this book to next semester's class.

10. Assume the role of a prosecuting attorney and put one of the characters from the book on trial for a crime. Prepare your case on paper, give all your arguments, and support them with facts from the book. Students working in groups may present the trial before the class, taking the roles of the accused, the judge, the defense attorney, the prosecuting attorney, and witnesses.

11. Create a game similar to Trivial Pursuit® or Pictionary® which reflects the details of your novel.

12. Create a high school yearbook with the main characters from the novel as graduating seniors. Clip out pictures from magazines or draw your own. Write a brief profile for each "senior" including the highlights of his or her school activities. Bind these pages as a book.

13. Design and create a "pop-up" book based on the text.

14. Write a telephone-answering-machine message for each major character in your book.

15. Write letters of recommendation for the major characters in your book.

16. Design your own response project. Plan it and have it approved by the teacher.

Name _____ Date _____

6.5   A Novel Response

Title of novel:_____

Author: _____

Number of pages: _____   My rating   1   2   3   4   5   6   7   8   9   10
                                              (low)   (high)

Characterization

1. Who is the main character? _____

2. What kind of person is the main character?

   Copy several sentences to support your statement.

3. List the things you liked best and those you liked least about the main character:

   Best:

   Least:

4. Compare yourself to one of the characters in the book. How are you alike or different?

5. Which character in the book changed the most? In what ways did he or she change?

6. Pretend you are the main character in the story. Write a brief description of another character from the main character's point of view.

Plot

7. In no more than fifty words, summarize the plot.

8. What is one problem in the story?

Which character has this problem?_____

What does he or she do to solve it?

9. Could the story have ended differently? Explain.

Setting

10. List as many words and phrases as you can find that tell where the story takes place.

11. Pretend you are one of the characters in the story. Complete this chart listing the sights, sounds, smells, tastes, and textures you experienced in the story.

sights	sounds	smells	tastes	textures

6.6   Responding to a Book

1. Why did you choose this book to read?

2. How did the author capture your interest as you began the book?

3. What did the author do to keep your interest as you read further?

4. Are there any similarities between this book and your own life? Explain.

5. What character would you like to be in this book? Explain

6. What would you and your favorite character talk about in your first conversation?

Begin the conversation:

7. Do you think the title fits the book? Why or why not?

8. What questions would you like answered after reading this book?

9. What seems to be the major point the author wants you to remember?

10. Who else should read this book? Why?

Who shouldn't read this book? Why?

Responses to Poetry

As you invite students to read and respond to poetry, it's especially important that you avoid questions like "What is this poet trying to say?" or "What is the hidden meaning in this poem?" Encourage students to be open to alternatives, and remind them to consider an entire poem, not just a line or phrase. Students should understand that a poem does not have to have a message. It may simply be someone's sharing of a view or a moment.

Questions for a poem.

1. How did this poem make you feel?
2. What idea is the author concerned about?
3. Does the poem make you aware of something you did not know before?
4. Are there any surprises in this poem?
5. What is the most important word in the poem?
6. What colors do you associate with the poem?
7. What sound do you associate with the poem?
8. What are some things that are puzzling to you about this poem? Did you solve any of the puzzles? Which ones and how?
9. What questions would you like to ask the poet? (Have each class member write one question he or she has about the poem and base an entire class discussion on students' questions.)

Responses *after* reading a poem.

1. Read a poem, then limit students' responses entirely to questions.
2. Rewrite some element of a poem in another format and compare the two. For example, after reading "Out, Out" by Robert Frost, students might write an obituary entry for the young boy in the poem and compare the two texts.
3. Draw an illustration for a poster and include the poem as a part of the presentation. Explain the relationship between the two.
4. Make a poem visual and help clarify its meaning by creating a mobile (that should balance when hung in the classroom).
5. Make a collection of favorite poems and bind these in a book to present to the school library. Include illustrations. (Books might also be based on themes such as nature, heroes and heroines, growing up.)
6. Keep a poetry journal. Include personal reactions and anything the poetry brings to mind.
7. Bring a picture to class that captures your response to a particular poem. As a whole-class assignment, request a picture from each student. Class discussion is based on the question of which picture the author might select for an illustration. If students work in groups, a reporter presents the group's choice to the class and explains and justifies this decision to the class.
8. Each day one student presents a written response to a poem. The subsequent

class discussion involves a reaction to both the student's response and the poem. Following each discussion, writers revise their papers, if necessary. Publish a class booklet of the revised writings.

9. Choose a poem and design a multimedia presentation about it to present to the class. The presentations should include costumes, props, or any additional material that will make the presentation effective (scent sprays, sound, and lighting, for example).

10. Create a collage representing the dominant impression of a piece.

11. Write a poem in the same style but on another subject.

12. Write a poem expressing the same point of view but in another style.

13. Write a letter to the poet sympathizing with the poet or arguing with the poet's point of view.

14. Choose a phrase or line in the poem and use it as a starting point for a personal writing.

15. Design, create, and model a poetry T-shirt. Using fabric paints, decorate a shirt with favorite published and personal poetry . Hold a "fashion show" and award prizes.[14]

The following assignment, 6.7 "Responding to Poetry," is an effective way to encourage students to interact with one another as they read and respond to poetry. The teacher's role is that of observer. Do not question, make comments, or become a part of a discussion. Sit back and allow students to function independently. They can handle this assignment successfully.

Name_____ Date _____

6.7   Responding to Poetry

In this poetry unit, you will be given a collection of poems. Read the poems and choose one that appeals to you. Register your choice with me. (If you have another poem in mind be sure you have it approved by me.) On scheduled days you will present your response to the poem you have chosen to the class as a whole. Plan for your response to take from 3 to 5 minutes. Responses should follow this format (but not necessarily in this order):

1. Indicate the title of your poem and its page number in the collection. (If you have obtained permission to use another poem, distribute copies to each class member.)

2. Read the poem to the class.

3. Call on someone to read the poem a second time. Plan ahead and be sure the person who does this is a willing, confident reader.

4. Present your response to the class.

5. Ask for comments, questions, and suggestions. Encourage students who have other observations about the poem to make their additions. Aim for a brief discussion period.

Types of responses to consider:

A. Create a list of at least fifteen thoughts that arise from the poem. Each sentence should begin with the phrase "I wonder. . ."

B. Write a several-paragraph response to the poem. Distribute carefully edited copies to each class member.

C. Write your own poem in response.

D. Write a monologue. Become a character from either inside or outside the poem. For example, if the poem is about a teenager, you might become that teenager or you could invent and become the teenager's parent, or principal, or teacher, for example. Distribute copies of the monologue to each person in the class.

E. Write a letter to someone about the poem and distribute copies to everyone.

F. Write a dialogue in response to the poem. Be sure each classmate has a copy.

G. Write a list of at least fifteen statements pointing out what you like about the poem. Each sentence will begin "I like . . ." Distribute copies.

H. Create and display a poster featuring both the poem and an illustration. Explain the relationship.

I. Make your poem into a mobile that balances when hung. Explain your reasoning and the process you followed in creating your response.

J. Create your own response.

Responding to Poetry, continued

The due date for your poetry response is _____, and it will be evaluated in the following manner:

First reading of poem (3)   _____

Second reading of poem (2)   _____

Presentation of your response to the class (10)   _____

Questions and comments elicited from the class (5) _____

Total (20)   _____

EVALUATION, TESTING, AND GRADING_____

Unfortunately, grades and tests often have the effect of undermining much of what we want to encourage and nurture in our classrooms—risk taking, exploration, and discovery. They often do little to help students learn something more about a subject, and they tend to label students rather than help them work from their strengths. Consider some of the following alternatives:

1. The students make out a set of examination questions based on their reading, and the teacher chooses questions from those submitted for the "real" test.

2. Let testing take a game format such as "Stump the Experts" or "Jeopardy®." Students working in groups write questions about a shared literary work and present their questions to other groups. In the "Jeopardy" format, contestants are given the answer and their response must be the correct question. In response to the study of a Shakespeare play, student questions might resemble the following:

Answers:	*Questions:*
1. Boy Actors	1. Who played women's parts in Shakespeare's plays?
2. Stratford-upon-Avon	2. What is Shakespeare's birthplace?

3. Ask students to write an exam including a short-answer section and an essay question for a text they have read. The students then take the exam themselves as they prepare an answer key.

4. Ask students to respond to a new text by using a familiar response. The multimedia presentation suggested earlier as response to a poem is a good activity for the end of a unit or grading period.

5. Require students to collect samples of their work over a period of time for a portfolio. The portfolio is a good alternative to traditional testing because it records a student's growth over time. (See Chapter 2 for a discussion of student portfolios.)

There is no single way to ensure student interest and involvement in literature. Don't hesitate, however, to try an occasional unorthodox technique that could help students approach literature creatively. Spend time talking with parents and administrators about what you and your students are doing in your classroom. Invite guests into the classroom for oral and dramatic activities or culminating projects. Think of yourself as an explorer and pay close attention to the students around you. Keep a journal or a record of what's occurring in your classroom. Don't ask too many questions to which you already know the answer, and involve students in lesson planning and problem solving. When something doesn't work, don't be afraid to ask, "What would make this better?" Then listen to your students' answers.

CHAPTER VII

Teaching Listening and Speaking

- *Teaching Listening*
- *Conversing with One Person*
- *Conversing in Small Groups*
- *Conversing in Large Groups*
- *Presenting Individual Speeches*

Teaching Listening and Speaking

My cousin is really smart. She was Val Victorian of her class.

The traditional approach to teaching the language arts has been to treat listening, speaking, reading, and writing as separate strands. Today, however, researchers and teachers point out that these are inextricably interrelated processes which are best taught integratively rather than separately.[1] This emphasis on the integration of speaking, listening, reading, and writing in the English classroom is a concern for many teachers who feel they lack the background and experience to teach listening and speaking skills in their classes. The good news is that if your students read and write together in response groups, they are already using all the language arts: They write a piece to bring before the group, read that piece, and listen to peer responses. Simultaneously, their peers listen, write responses, and react orally. If you also encourage your students to respond to literature in a variety of ways both written and oral—independently, in small-group discussions, and in oral presentations to the class—they are also practicing listening and speaking skills.

Despite the fact that you are providing plenty of opportunities for speaking and listening in your classroom, you also want your students to become more skillful speakers and listeners. The following is a discussion of a variety of activities that will help you teach these skills as your students read and write together.[2]

TEACHING LISTENING

Although our students may spend the greatest portion of their class time listening, many have become efficient at not listening at all. To many, listening means being quiet and paying passive attention to the teacher. As teachers, we realize how much one's success in society depends on the ability to listen and speak well. We want our students to become active, involved listeners who will become articulate members of society. Consider using one or more of the following activities as you introduce a brief listening unit early in the year. Each lesson will take approximately one class period.

Lesson 1.

1. Introduce the familiar game "telephone." One person (a student or the teacher) begins by turning to the next student and quietly relaying a short spoken phrase or set of directions. This is passed along to each member of the

class. The last student to receive the information repeats the message he or she has heard to the entire class, and this is compared with the original. Naturally, the messages undergo interesting evolutions as they are passed along. Students have fun, and the exercise makes a strong argument for the necessity of paying attention.

2. Direct everyone to sit quietly for two or three minutes and mentally make a list of all the sounds they hear:

> "Close your eyes and focus your attention on what you hear.
> Keep listening for everything: sounds in the distance and
> sounds up close—even your own breathing."

After the time has elapsed, ask students to contribute to a list of words naming the sounds they have heard. Define *onomatopoeia* (words that imitate the sounds they name), and point out examples of these words as you record them on the blackboard.

3. Pair students. Direct each to carry on a quiet conversation with a partner with their eyes closed. Suggest that they pay close attention to each word of the partner. Notice the tone, volume, and pace of the partner's voice. Check to see if the words are in complete sentences or in short fragments. At the end of the conversations, ask the pairs to respond to this experience either as a freewriting or orally. Many are likely to say they felt closer to the partner as they really listened to the other person, undistracted by other sounds and their own thoughts. Point out that the best listener pays close attention and shows respect for the speaker's words.[3]

4. Locate a recording of a song to which the students would not know the words (an "oldie," for example). It is best if you can provide the actual written lyrics. Play the song once without interruption while the students write down as many of the lyrics as possible. Then play the piece again, pausing after lines to allow students time to write. Finally, hand out the actual lyrics so that students can see if they listened correctly and play the song again. Discuss the need for concentration and purpose when listening.[4]

Lesson 2.

1. Pair students.

2. One member of each pair moves his or her desk to face the blackboard. The second student moves his or her desk to face away from the board. The student facing the board is the "speaker," and the student facing away is the "listener."

3. Tape to the board a sketch similar to one of the following:

4. The speaker describes the sketch to the listener who (without looking at the board) reproduces it on a piece of notebook paper. The listener cannot talk or ask questions, but concentrates on listening as carefully as possible to the speaker's instructions. The speaker should not look at the listener's sketch.

5. When each sketch is completed, ask the students to compare theirs to the original.

6. Have the partners exchange roles and try the exercise again with another figure.[5]

7. Ask each pair to evaluate their efforts as speakers and listeners.

Lesson 3.

1. Explain that the day's activities are concerned with listening and the characteristics of good listeners.

2. Ask students to find a partner they do not know well. (If there is an uneven number of students, you should become someone's partner.)

3. Write a series of topics for discussion on the blackboard. For example:

   • What is it like to grow up in a small town, a large city, a close-knit neighborhood ? (choose one)
   • The proudest moment of my life and why.
   • What I'd like to accomplish in my life and why.
   • My greatest fear and why.
   • Pick a topic of your own.

4. Direct one student in each pair to speak with his or her partner on a chosen topic for three to five minutes. The second student is to listen and encourage the speaker.

5. After the time has elapsed, students exchange roles for another three to five minutes.

6. For a brief time (45 seconds to 1 minute), students again exchange roles as they continue with the original topic or discuss a new one. This time tell the students acting as listeners to give negative feedback.

7. Repeat

8. In a round-the-room session, ask the following questions:

   a. What did your partner do to encourage you as a speaker?
   b. What did your partner do to discourage you as a speaker?
   c. Tell us one new bit of information you learned about your partner.

9. Ask everyone to contribute to a definition of good and bad listeners. Record the suggestions on the blackboard. These may resemble the following:

   a. Good listeners
      • are supportive and kind
      • let the speaker know they hear what is being said
      • ask useful, interesting questions

- show they are interested
- look at the speaker

b. Poor listeners
- interrupt
- criticize or argue
- concentrate on another activity
- speak to someone else

Throughout the year, continue to emphasize active listening skills. Make a practice of giving oral instructions carefully and clearly—but give them only once. Answer any questions about the meaning of the instructions, but don't repeat the instructions. At first students may grumble about this policy, but they will quickly become more attentive listeners.

Encourage students who are not part of an oral presentation to practice good listening skills. Following an oral presentation, have each write a brief summary or a list of main ideas. This assignment need not become an extra correcting burden for you. Simply give every student a few points for having done the summary or call on a few students to read their summaries aloud while you comment on them orally. For more formal speaking activities, expect all students to respond on an evaluation form.

CONVERSING WITH ONE PERSON

The most common person-to-person communication in many language arts classrooms takes place between you and a student in a writing conference. It also happens easily between two students who are deliberately paired off to interview one other, to act as peer editors for one another's writing, or to brainstorm together.

Rehearsals

As a prewriting activity, encourage your students to explain their writing plans to their partners. This is sometimes called "rehearsing" a writing. As the author explains what he or she intends to say, the topic becomes more focused. The partner's questions also help the writer clarify his or her goals. Talking about writing is also a good speaking and listening activity because students don't know it's an exercise and their conversation is relaxed and spontaneous.

Focused Discussions

At the beginning of a class, pose two or three open-ended questions pertaining to the day's reading assignment. Display the questions on an overhead transparency or write them on the blackboard. Ask students to work independently to answer each question. Next, have students work in pairs to share and compare answers with their partners. Remind everyone to listen carefully to the partners' answers and explanations. Finally, ask each pair to create a new answer which is superior to their initial individual answers. Collect only the pairs' final effort. These may be graded or used as a springboard for further class discussion.[6]

Interviews

Because we live in an information age, the ability to acquire information is one of the most important skills we can teach our students. In addition to knowing how to do library research, our students should understand that information can also be acquired from expert testimony. Interviewing skills, which can be practiced and learned, are invaluable for every student in our classrooms.

Preparation for an interview is important. A student who will conduct an interview should:

- research the subject to be able to ask good questions;
- choose an opening question and organize follow-up questions;
- avoid questions which can be answered "yes" or "no";
- ask follow-up questions for clarification;
- restate answers to ensure an understanding of what has been said;
- persist politely to get needed information; and
- take good notes.

As a part of a year-long course design, structure a series of practice interviewing exercises such as the following:

Activity 1.

As an opening class activity, pair students and ask each to consider a single question, such as

- What television commercial do you like best (or least)? Why?
- If you could meet any person living today, who would you meet and why?
- What is the title of a novel you could recommend to other students in this class? Why?
- What is the most dangerous thing you have ever done?

Students interview one another and report what they have learned to the class as a whole.

Activity 2.

Use improvisational role playing activities to develop interviewing skills. For example, place slips of paper in a container naming types of people such as doctor, dentist, author, someone from history, a character in a well-known story. One student in a pair draws out a slip. After time for brainstorming, the second student interviews the partner as if the partner were the character named on the slip.

Activity 3.

Structure activities so that the students must acquire information through interviews to share with the class. For example, before a research project, give specific students or students working in groups the responsibility of finding out how to use particular resources in the library. Students interview the librarian and report orally to the class. (This could also result in a written set of directions for using the source.)

Activity 4.

As part of a particular unit, invite a community expert into your classroom. Instead of having the expert deliver a lecture or give a talk, structure the visit so that students must obtain information by interviewing the guest. A variation of this activity is to ask several guests to visit the classroom at the same time. Students are appointed to small groups, and the guests take turns being interviewed by each of the small groups in a round-robin.

Activity 5.

Research projects may be based on interviews. For example, students interview a family member or interesting person in the community and write a personality profile. Collect the profiles in a polished class publication. Projects such as this also involve letter writing (a request for an interview, a confirmation letter, and a thank-you letter) in addition to plenty of cooperative planning for editing and publishing the booklet. (The I-Search paper discussed in Chapter 5 also relies heavily on interviews.) Form 7.1, "Guide for an Interview," is helpful for students as they prepare for such an interview.

7.1   Guide for an Interview

1. The name of the person I plan to interview is:_____

2. The topic of my interview is: _____

3. Read up on this topic. List as much as you know about this subject:

4. Think about the preceding list. Now begin a new list. What do you want to find out?

5. Decide on an opening question. Write it here.

6. Make a list of questions for your interview on the back of this sheet. Remember:

   A. Questions should be open-ended, not the kind that can be answered by a yes or no. For example: "Did you decide to become a lawyer for the money?" Better: "Why did you decide to become a lawyer?"

   B. Questions should be specific, not general. Example: "What is your opinion on the law and teenagers?" Better: "Does the law treat teenagers differently than adults?"

   C. Ask for the facts. For example: "Tell me about capital punishment." Better: "Under what circumstances might a teenage criminal be treated as an adult?"

During the interview, listen carefully and always ask for more detail. Jot down the answers as quickly as you can, without worrying about spelling or punctuation. Give the person whom you are interviewing plenty of time to talk. Don't interrupt or tell your own stories or stick so close to your list of questions that you miss what the person is saying. If something interesting comes up, follow that line of thought, but keep in mind the purpose of your interview. People are interesting. They will give you good information and tell you wonderful stories if you give them the chance.

CONVERSING IN SMALL GROUPS

Cooperative Skills

Many experts suggest that small-group work is one of the most important processes to happen in our classrooms. They point out that students are challenged to define, clarify, qualify, elaborate, analyze, and develop the thinking and verbalizing skills needed for reading and writing.[7] (See Chapter 4 for a complete discussion of cooperative learning activities.) It's important, however, to remember that our students seldom have the social skills needed to converse effectively in groups. They must learn to:

- value the contributions of all group members;
- take turns speaking;
- listen to other speakers;
- disagree with another student's words without criticizing the speaker;
- respond to the previous speaker;
- organize a group to meet a goal; and
- encourage others to join in.

Whenever students work in groups, observe and monitor them. Reserve time at the end of each group activity to discuss your observations, emphasizing what each group has done well. Ask students to evaluate their own performances. In our busy schedules, it's tempting to skip this part of the lesson, but it's something you must not do. Your students can and will learn to function well in groups if you give them the opportunity to regularly assess their performance.

Gender Differences

As we plan for listening and speaking activities in our classrooms, we intend to make the kinds of classroom decisions that are best for all our students. One concern we may have is equal treatment of boys and girls. For example, researchers point out that when boys and men talk with one another in all-male groups, they often compete for dominance and assert their status by the length of time they keep the floor, and interruptions or hostile comments are frequently seen as normal interaction. Males tend to ignore the comments of previous speakers and usually make strongly assertive statements. They also tend to play the devil's advocate and seldom reveal personal thoughts or feelings. Men tend to speak at the lower end of their speaking range, and in this culture, the lower range is the one that carries authority.[8]

Girls and women, on the other hand, are more likely to support a speaker by providing reinforcements such as positive comments or nonverbal cues such as head nods. If a woman interrupts a speaker, this is not seen as an attempt to gain the floor, but is more likely to be a request for elaboration. Women are more likely to make an effort to get everyone in the group to participate. In speaking, women tend to make false starts, use a questioning intonation when making a statement, have hesitant pacing, and use an excessive number of qualifiers. Women tend to speak at the higher end of their speaking range.[9]

There are implications in all this for our classroom. We are told teachers tend to value class contributions delivered in the assertive "male style" regardless of content and to penalize lack of participation in discussion. We need to be aware of this. We also need to be alert to classroom dynamics. If, for example, certain boys consistently dominate class discussions, we can insist that all students spend two or three minutes thinking over the question or topic before a discussion is initiated. We can ensure that both sexes get practice asking both supportive and challenging questions. We can encourage slower, louder, and lower speaking in those who tend to be uncertain and high-pitched. We can stress the value of listening and we can design activities that call for both cooperative and competitive activities.

In addition to the cooperative activities discussed in Chapter 4, consider using small-group discussions in the following ways:

Embedded Discussions

Embedded discussions are those which can be used within another activity. For example, an entire class may study a novel. In place of a large-group discussion, appoint students to small groups and give each group its own open-ended question. The small group decides upon a recorder and reporter and discusses its question for a specified time. Finally, the reporter for each group reports to the class as a whole. For example, if a class were discussing *To Kill a Mockingbird,* you might devise group questions such as the following:

- Define *mockingbird* and explain which characters might be thought of as mockingbirds.

- One of the themes in this novel is "getting into someone's skin" to understand him or her. Which characters in this novel do this or should do this? Explain.

- The author places limitations on the narrator's ability to tell the story. What are they? What is their purpose?

- Scout grows up in this novel. How does she change and what does she learn?

Panel Discussions

Small-group discussions are excellent preparation for more formal panel discussions later in the year. A panel discussion is an excellent format for involving students in library research, cooperative work, and oral presentations without the grading burden of the traditional research paper. Students are assigned to groups of four or no more than five, and each group brainstorms a list of topics the members are interested in researching (the early history of their community, for example). Once the group has agreed upon a topic and received your approval of the topic, members begin their research, breaking the general topic into subtopics for which individual students are responsible. Whenever necessary, you will teach mini-lessons pertaining to research tools, summary writing, note taking, and interviewing. Finally, after the library research has been completed and school and community experts have been interviewed, each student prepares his or her information for the group's oral presentation to the class. Students should understand that they may consult notes as they speak but they should not read from a script. Group members help one another as they practice and rehearse their oral presentations. Finally, each group makes its presentation to the entire class. Although there are many variations, the usual format for a panel discussion is:

1. Opening remarks by the group's moderator including an explanation of the topic and the reasons for the group's choice of the topic, for example.

2. Introduction of speakers by the moderator along with an explanation of the subtopics.

3. Presentations by members of the panel

4. Audience participation, usually in the form of questions to panel members.

5. Conclusion or summary by the moderator.

In addition, you may also ask each group to submit a bibliography. Although it involves more reading and grading on your part, you may also ask students to submit individual summaries of their research. Ideally, you will award both individual and group grades.

Cooperative Controversies

As teachers, we are reminded we need to provide a framework in which our students can think and work and listen and speak, and then we must back away, encourage their opinions, and avoid playing the expert. The following activity known as a *cooperative controversy* encourages this to happen. It is an ideal activity to couple with a unit concerning library research and /or interviewing. In addition, it does not create an unmanageable paper load.

1. Arrange students in groups of four.

2. Direct groups to brainstorm for a topic based on controversies they see in their school or community. A sample list might resemble the following:

   - Progress being made in recycling in our community is too slow.
   - A pass-fail grading system should be adopted in our school.
   - Our school should have an open campus.
   - Adopted children should be encouraged to find their birth parents.

3. After each group has decided on a topic, assign half of the students in each group to the pro side and half to the con side of the question.

4. Students conduct library research and interview experts. All members of the group collaborate by sharing information about the issue in one or several strategy sessions.

5. On a specified date, the small groups convene to present the information each has gathered to others in their small group. When the pro side presents its arguments, the con side records them. When the con side presents its arguments, the pro side makes a record of these arguments.

6. The sides are switched, and the groups meet again in strategy and research sessions.

7. The new pro side presents its arguments, and the new con side records them. The new con side presents its arguments, and the new pro side records these.

8. Finally, each group works together to consider and discuss what has been learned and to write , either individually or as a group, a report that includes a balanced discussion of both sides of the controversy and all supporting evidence.[10]

Asking students to look at issues from more than one point of view helps them move away from rigid, preconceived positions. The small-group format encourages students to actively think, learn, speak, and listen to produce well-reasoned and well-documented writing.

Group Improvisations

Stories are everywhere, and students can and should be encouraged to create, expand, and improvise stories in a variety of ways.

1. The entire class may be involved in a group story. One student is asked to begin the story. In a round-robin, every other class member contributes one sentence to the story, which is ended by the last student. Stories can be fun and silly, but with practice students get better and better at this, and a cohesive plot and story structure emerge.

2. Pair students. The first student begins telling a story, but when the teacher says "stop," the second student continues the story. The two continue to take turns telling the story as directed to do so by the teacher. This can also be used as a writing exercise and works especially well with word processors. Pairs who first write their stories should also be asked to read them aloud.

3. Read an unfamiliar story to the class but stop before the ending. Groups collaborate in brainstorming, writing, and acting out an ending. After the last version is presented, conduct a whole-class discussion about the different versions.

4. Suggest story endings such as "Finally, he knocked on the door", or "She picked up the phone", or "She said 'I stole the jackknife' ." Groups brainstorm, create, and enact a complete story.

5. Place face down on a table a collection of photographs which feature groups of people. Each group draws one picture from the collection. Groups brainstorm, create, and enact a story based on their picture.[11]

6. Read a summary account of a scene to each group or invite a group to invent its own. Summary accounts involve the three w's: Who is in the scene? Where is the scene? What is the relationship? ("An old man who has just lost five dollars meets a ten-year-old boy in the park," or "A thirteen-year-old girl oversleeps, but her mother still insists she go to school," are summary accounts.) Groups brainstorm about possibilities for each scene, expand on the story, and enact it for the class.

7. Assign each group a specific setting—taxi cab, elevator, emergency room, theater lobby, or supermarket checkout line, for example. Group members decide what type of person each will represent (driver, executive, doctor, traveler from abroad, farmer, child, parent) and improvise a scene.

8. Place single words printed on separate cards in a container. Individuals or groups draw a card and tell a story suggested by the word on the card. A variation of this exercise is to fill a bag with a collection of found objects. Each student or group draws one object and tells a story based on that object.

9. A group selects a character it has studied in a piece of literature during the year. It then writes and performs a skit which places this character in a contemporary setting and reflects the theme or idea in the original work. (One of the boys in *Lord of the Flies* may work at an American fast-food restaurant, for example.)

CONVERSING IN LARGE GROUPS

A good class discussion is actually a conversation with much interaction taking place among students as they share different points of view. The immediacy of responding to and questioning each other is not possible in writing, so class discussion can make the literature your students read and study especially meaningful. The following suggestions will help you foster successful large-group discussion:

1. Seat students in a large circle so that every student can see every other person in the room.

2. From time to time, choose student leaders. Discussions are often more honest when students lead them.

3. Ask students to generate a list of questions pertaining to the topic before the discussion begins. Choose those questions that offer the most possibilities. Base the subsequent discussion on these student-generated questions.

4. Have students freewrite about a question before discussing it. This gives all students equal time to think about a topic, and discussions are often better because students have thought the question through. If you do not plan to have students write before a discussion, allow plenty of "wait time" following a question to give an opportunity for reflection.

5. Discourage interruptions, wild hand-waving, and distractions when someone is speaking. Students should volunteer by raising their hands, but also call on those who don't. Occasionally, give participation points based solely on the number of times a student responds, but point out that the best discussions include contributions from everyone.

6. Keep a record of who has spoken. This can be as simple as a check next to a student's name on a seating chart. A student can serve as a monitor, as well. We need to do this because we tend to think we have called on many more students than we actually have. If a student tends to monopolize every class discussion, let him or her act as a monitor occasionally. Another option is to begin the discussion period by giving each student two or three "speaker's tickets." Explain that once students have spent their tickets, they cannot speak again until all others have spent theirs.

7. Don't let the "I don't know" student off the hook. Rephrase the question, ask for a personal response, or come back to the student later in the discussion. Gentle persistence with this type of student will pay off over time.

8. Acknowledge a speaker in some way. Although you will want to avoid making comments that evaluate students' responses, you need to let them know you have heard. "What do you mean by . . .?" or "Can you give me some examples?" are the types of responses which are helpful.

9. Plan for closure at the end of a class discussion. For example, ask students to turn to a partner and do one of the following:

- Point out two important points raised in the discussion.
- Comment on an idea in the discussion that was interesting or thought provoking.
- Suggest one question that still has not been answered.

The partner discussion further ensures that every class member is involved. One member of each pair may report to the class as a whole.

PRESENTING INDIVIDUAL SPEECHES————————————

Formal speeches by individual students to the entire class can be enormously time consuming. While it is possible to divide your classes into smaller groups so that several speeches can be given at one time, this means finding three or four rooms if they are available and videotaping the speeches so you can evaluate them. If you teach in a school where you cannot leave students unsupervised, it is also possible to recruit parent volunteers. The logistics of all of this is discouraging. On the other hand, we're usually not happy with the one-speech-per-semester approach, and we fear that such a requirement tends to reinforce students' apprehension about public speaking.

The following are short, less threatening activities that encourage individuals to speak frequently without creating an overwhelming logistical or grading burden for you.

Announcements

Announcements usually include information about who, what, where, when, and sometimes why and how. If students have this information, they can be and should be responsible for making all classroom announcements. For practice, they can have fun inventing announcements, too. Invented announcements are particularly good for involving shy or reluctant students.

Simile

Brief speeches based on comparisons encourage students to reveal something about themselves as they learn about this literary device.

1. Begin with a class discussion of what a simile is: a comparison between two unlike things using "like" or "as." In this instance students would compare themselves to any real or fictional thing except another person.
2. Provide samples: "My life is like a winding journey," or "She acts like a thorny bush."
3. The introduction includes the speaker's name and the object of comparison. ("My name is Jane and I'm like a house cat.")
4. The simile is supported by two main points that explain the comparison. ("I am independent and like to sleep a lot. I am affectionate and loving to my family when I am around them.")
5. The concluding sentence restates the first.[12]

Introductions

Point out the rules of formal introductions and provide opportunities for your students to practice these in your classroom. Traditional introduction guidelines are as follows:

1. Determine whose status is lesser or greater by age (older people have more status) and by position, rank, or job (presidents, principals, generals, and so forth).

2. Introduce a person of lesser status to a person of greater status.

3. State the name of the higher-ranking person first.

4. The person making the introduction should provide a conversation opener such as an item of mutual interest the two individuals share.

5. The person of greater status extends his or her hand first if there is a handshake. The person of lesser status does not extend a hand if the higher-ranking person does not.

6. One should establish eye contact with the person to whom one is being introduced.

7. A person of lesser status always rises, if seated, and the person of greater status should also rise as a mark of friendship.

8. The two build on the conversation starter to continue the conversation.

Activities for Introductions.

1. Direct students to write on a slip of paper the name of a person living or dead, real or fictional, famous or ordinary. They should also include the person's age, job, or rank. Collect the slips in a container and have each draw one and introduce the person named on the slip to the class.

2. Turn interviews with student partners into introductions to the class. If the class is large or the students seem especially insecure about speaking in front of the whole class, form groups of six or eight for practice before beginning the whole class activity.

3. Select characters from a piece of familiar literature and call on students to introduce each to the whole class. This is an excellent activity prior to writing more formal character descriptions based on the literature.

4. Expect your students to introduce classroom guests to the class. This will involve some interviewing skills, as well.

Directions

Exercises and practice in giving both written and oral directions help students to understand and use precise language. Simple class activities can lead to more formal demonstration speeches. Begin by providing information about the nature of directions:

- Directions are usually given in chronological order.
- If they are lengthy, directions may be organized in segments or steps.
- If manipulatives are involved, practice is important.
- The speaker states the benefit of being able to follow the directions.
- The conclusion is usually a summary and a reminder of the usefulness of the information.

Activity 1: Drawing.

A. Students are paired.

B. One student draws a simple design and gives the partner oral or written directions for drawing the same design.

C. The second student follows the directions to produce a similar design.

C. The students compare the two designs.

Activity 2: Movement.

A. Pair students. One student is blindfolded.

B. The second student accompanies the blindfolded student and gives him or her oral directions for getting from the classroom to another location in the building.

C. The students exchange roles.

D. The partners discuss and define the characteristics of effective directions.

Activity 3. How To.

A. A student talks a partner through an unfamiliar procedure, such as how to do origami, knit, make an art project, play a game such as "4 square," compute square roots, or build a model out of Legos.

B. An interesting variation is to place a barrier between the two students so they can hear each other but cannot see each other.

Demonstrations

Using how-to books checked out of the library or based on skills they already know, students demonstrate a skill to the class. Demonstrations, with oral explanations, might include setting up a tent, decorating a cake, crocheting, riding a horse, using the proper techniques for operating shop tools, or applying CPR, for example. Teaching a skill or concept (such as finger plays or songs) to younger students is another good approach.

Alternatives to Book Reports

As a response to a reading and literature unit based on biographies, students become the subjects of their biographies. Wearing self-designed costumes and using simple props, each presents an oral narrative based on his or her reading. The following is a helpful format for this project:

- family background
- formal/informal education
- contributions to humankind
- impact on society[13]

The same approach may also be used with fiction by asking students to talk about their book from the point of view of one of its main characters. Form 7.2, "Oral Report on a Book," is an evaluation form for such an activity. Encourage the listeners in the class to complete an evaluation form as well.

7.2   Oral Report on a Book

Scale: 1 = weak, 2 = fair, 3 = average, 4 = good, 5 = excellent

1. content	1	2	3	4	5
2. volume	1	2	3	4	5
3. rate	1	2	3	4	5
4. enunciation	1	2	3	4	5
5. costume	1	2	3	4	5
6. props	1	2	3	4	5

Comments:

Total possible: 30 points

Your score: _____

Evaluator: _____

Reading and Storytelling

Impromptu reading in the classroom may happen occasionally, but taking turns around the room can be deadly. Instead, as part of your lesson design, have students select excerpts from a piece of literature and study and rehearse the selection to read to the class. Such a project works well with a poetry unit, for example.

Invite a storyteller from the community into the classroom to model formal storytelling. Students should understand an effective storyteller is concerned with the rate, volume, and pitch of the voice as well as the physical aspects of facial expression, gesture, and eye contact. A good storyteller will create distinct voices for each character. After observing an expert storyteller, students can be expected to create and practice their own stories and deliver them to an audience in a variety of ways: cassette tape, puppet theater, videotape, or "live." "Readers' Theater" is an excellent extension of this. Student-written plays, stories, and poems can be prepared and delivered to audiences outside the classroom—to other classrooms, PTA meetings, or student assemblies, for example. Students should practice their stories in small groups prior to a whole-class activity. See form 7.3 "Storytelling Evaluation."

Name_____ Date _____

7.3 Storytelling Evaluation

Scale: 1 = weak, 2 = fair, 3 = average, 4 = good, 5 = excellent

Vocal

rate	1	2	3	4	5
volume	1	2	3	4	5
pitch	1	2	3	4	5

Physical

facial expression	1	2	3	4	5
gestures	1	2	3	4	5
eye contact	1	2	3	4	5

Characterizations	1	2	3	4	5
General impression	1	2	3	4	5

Comments:

Total possible: 40 points

Your score: _____

Evaluator: _____

Speeches to Inform or Persuade

Assignments that require students to inform or persuade can consume a great deal of class time if they are made as separate assignments. However, in an integrated classroom it is possible to ask students to prepare speeches in conjunction with other assignments. For example, if students have completed an I-Search or research paper or a cooperative controversy, they are well prepared on a subject. It's logical to consider assigning an informative or persuasive speech as a follow-up assignment. An evaluation form for these speeches is suggested in form 7.4, "Evaluation Form for an Informative or Persuasive Speech."

Additional Suggestions

Students need to have many successful oral experiences early in a course to build confidence for more challenging speaking assignments. Discussions with partners, conversations in small groups, impromptu group exercises, and whole-group round-robin exercises give students the experience and confidence for more formal speaking activities. Assignments that encourage students to incorporate costumes or props such as maps, charts, or pictures are especially successful for shy students who are reluctant to speak before a group.

Early on, de-emphasize the importance of grades. If grades must be given for a formal activity, devise a checklist or grading grid for each assignment. Encourage your students to rehearse in small groups before speaking to the entire class, and involve every class member in the subsequent evaluation.

Name _____ Date _____

7.4 Evaluation Form for an Informative or Persuasive Speech

Scale: 1 = weak, 2 = fair, 3 = average, 4 = good, 5 = excellent

Introduction

captures the audience's attention	1	2	3	4	5
provides background information	1	2	3	4	5

Body

presents information clearly	1	2	3	4	5
makes information interesting	1	2	3	4	5
uses supporting evidence	1	2	3	4	5

Conclusion

summarizes main points	1	2	3	4	5

Delivery

uses effective vocal delivery (volume, rate, quality)	1	2	3	4	5
uses effective physical delivery (eye contact, facial expression, gestures)	1	2	3	4	5

Responses to questions

clarity of answers	1	2	3	4	5

Comments:

Total possible: 45 points

Your score: _____

Evaluator: _____

CHAPTER VIII

Working with Others

- *Working with Parents*
- *Working with Teachers and Administrators*
- *Working with Community Resources*

Working with Others

I'm sorry about the way I talked to you yesterday, Mrs. B.
I still think you were wrong , though, and so does my mother.

Wwe work in a setting filled with active, energetic adolescents. We're surrounded by fellow teachers, administrators, and support staff. There are only rare moments during the day that we can truly call our own. And yet one of the most common complaints from teachers is a sense of loneliness and isolation, a sense of "going it alone." We spend seven to eight hours each day in the small area known as our classroom and seldom see the teachers on the other end of the building. We wonder about the experiences our students have in other classes across the curriculum, and we know we are in touch with too few parents. We hope for a sense of community, a feeling of working as a team because we want the best for our students and ourselves. We work to become better teachers and seek validation that we're teaching well. We believe many good things are happening in education across the nation, and we want to make the same happen in our schools. Fortunately, there is much we can do to work toward these goals.

WORKING WITH PARENTS

Every study that has ever been done concerning parental involvement shows that students do better in school when their parents are involved in their education.[1] Some parents will gladly give you the support you need, some want to help but don't know how, some are angry at schools in general, and some just don't seem to care. Though parents and their situations may differ, you can work to make each parent a positive factor in contributing to a student's success in your classroom. Consider using some of the following strategies as you work to increase parental involvement.

Beginning of the Year

Don't wait until a problem occurs to contact parents. Begin working even before the school year gets under way to gain their support. Mail a postcard greeting to all parents and incoming students before the first day of school. Keep the message simple and upbeat. Introduce yourself, and let your students and their parents know you are looking forward to the year and working together. The message can be as simple as the following:

To the family of _____,

I was pleased to learn _____ will be a student in my
English classroom this fall. I am looking forward to a wonderful year, and
I hope you are, too.

Sincerely,

On one of the first days of school, have each student address an envelope. Then mail each parent a letter introducing yourself and your class. Form 8.1, "Sample Letter to Parents," is useful in this regard.

8.1   Sample Letter to Parents

To the parents of _____,

My name is _____ , and I will be your child's English teacher this year. I am looking forward to the coming school year and am pleased _____ will be in my classroom. I believe that it is important for parents and teachers to work together to ensure the best education possible for each student. I encourage you to visit our classroom and to contact me whenever you have a comment, question, or suggestion. Please phone the school office at _____ , and I will respond as quickly as possible. I look forward to a happy and successful year as we work together.

Sincerely,

I have read the above letter. I can be reached at_____

The best time to phone is_____

Parent/Guardian's Name (please print) _____

Parent/Guardian's Signature _____

Student's Name (please print) _____

Date _____

Comments:

You can also include additional information in your introductory letter. For example:

- educational philosophy
- class requirements
- grading system
- homework policy
- list of materials the student will be reading
- major projects and deadlines
- students' responsibilities

If the cost of mailing these letters is prohibitive, ask the students to deliver them to their parents, and include a student bonus-point coupon or a tear-off sheet that parents sign and return. Provide a space for comments and any additional information that will be helpful to you.

Back-to-School Night and Parents' Workshops

A Back-to-School Night can be one of the most important events of the school year because it is your single best opportunity to meet parents, explain your policies and program in detail, answer questions about your class, and emphasize the importance of parental involvement in students' learning. Unfortunately, parents of older students aren't as likely to attend as those of younger students. There are, however, some things you can do to increase attendance. Involve your students in decorating the classroom, posting welcome signs, and designing and delivering invitations. Generate enthusiasm they can pass along to their parents. Form 8.2, "Sample Invitation", is a simple format that can be further decorated and personalized by each student. An R.S.V.P. tear-off sheet will help commit parents to attendance. You might also feature a raffle drawing or offer bonus points for students whose parents do attend.

8.2 A Sample Invitation to Back-to-School Night

An Invitation

To:_____

You're invited to a Back-to-School Night.

Place: _____

Date: _____

Time: _____

Please join us for Back-to-School Night to meet
the teachers, visit classrooms, and learn what
you can do to help your child have a successful
school year. I'm looking forward to meeting
you and explaining our class plans and goals for the
coming year. Do plan to attend.

- -

____ I will be attending.

____ I won't be attending.

Name _____

Parent of _____

It's important that you carefully plan your Back-to School Night presentation to parents. This is not a time to talk about individual students but rather to explain your educational philosophy and to discuss general information which will be helpful to every parent. The following format will help you organize an effective presentation:

1. Introduce yourself.
2. Welcome everyone and stress the significant role parents play in their son's or daughter's academic success.
3. Explain your academic program for the semester (or year). Mention major assignments and important deadlines.
4. Stress the importance of good attendance.
5. Briefly describe your discipline plan.
6. Describe your homework policy.
7. Explain your grading policy.
8. Explain how parents can help their students at home and request their support. Form 8.3, "Twelve Ways Parents Can Help Their Kids Succeed in High School," offers excellent advice and may be reproduced and distributed to parents.
9. Ask for questions and suggestions.
10. End on a positive note. Emphasize the importance of parents and teachers working together for the success of each student.

8.3 Twelve Ways Parents Can Help Their Kids Succeed in High School*

Here are twelve ways to help your child succeed in high school:

1. Encourage your child to ride the bus. Even though bus transportation is provided for high school students, school parking lots are filled to overflowing with student-driven cars. A frequent excuse for first-hour tardiness is "car trouble." Not only do tardy students lose valuable learning time at the start of the class, but they interrupt the learning atmosphere and take up administration and teacher time. Bus transportation is reliable, on time, safe, and free.

2. Try to schedule family vacations when school is not in session. When students miss a week or more it is almost impossible to make up learning experiences. Also, considerable teacher time is taken up on makeup work.

3. Give some thought to the sacrifices in student time and energy because of car ownership. Many students put in considerable time on jobs to support cars. Students tired from evening jobs are not at their best and are often unable to put in the time to complete homework and study for tests.

4. Provide your child with an assignment book, such as a business appointment book. Ask your child to enter due dates of projects, homework assignments, tests, and other obligations and events. Expect your child to keep the book up to date and ask to see it from time to time. Students will find assignment books a valuable tool for time management.

5. The kitchen table may be the best place for doing homework. A surprising number of high school students have a television and a telephone in their rooms. Do not assume that time spent in their rooms "doing homework" is not also spent watching television and talking on the phone. Doing homework at the kitchen table allows parents to observe student work and discuss assignments.

6. Help your child plan his or her school program. Your input is valuable in class selection and career choices. Your child will appreciate your interest and judgment. Also, parents' serious attitude toward education is transmitted to children. Attitude is often more important than ability when it comes to success at school.

7. Try to have at least one adult at home during the evening. Although difficult, any juggling of schedules that achieves better parental supervision and knowledge of how adolescents spend their time is well worth the effort. Students who come to school rested, properly attired, and well nourished are truly ready to learn.

8. Help your child set reasonable academic goals at the beginning of each year and grading period. Discuss the child's progress from time to time and update or review goals together. When grades come out, review goals in relation to grades. If the student does not achieve the goals, try to determine why. Be realistic in your expectations, offer plenty of encouragement, and most important, praise your child for a job well done.

© 1994 by The Center for Applied Research in Education

---

* "Twelve Ways Parents Can Help Their Kids Succeed in High School" by Robert E. Knudson, Roseville, English Teacher, Mounds View High School, St. Paul, Minnesota, 1992, used by permission.

9. When in doubt, check it out. Student perceptions of incidents and events at school often differ markedly from those of the adults at school. When you have a concern, call the school and ask to speak with the person you think is best able to help you. If teachers are in class, leave a message and they will return your call. Such calls often clear up issues and prevent small problems from becoming big ones.

10. In 60 percent of American homes not a single book was bought last year, yet there are more televisions in the United States than there are households. Provide books, magazines, and newspapers. Set a good example by reading. And, though it may come as a surprise, even high school students love to be read to aloud.

11. See that your child has breakfast. Studies have shown that children of all ages do better in school if they eat breakfast.

12. Remember that you are a key figure on your child's educational team. Trust your own judgment and common sense. Don't be too hard on yourself when things don't go quite as you hoped, and keep your sense of humor. No one person is responsible for your child's success in school. A team effort is the most successful approach.

You may find that the people you want most to attend are the ones who don't. Consider sending a follow-up note to these parents, summarizing your information and again encouraging them to contact you with any questions, concerns, or suggestions.

In addition to a Back-to-School Night, encourage your colleagues to host a departmental workshop for parents. Involve the entire English department. Send invitations and invite parents to learn more about the department and the language-arts curriculum. Introduce staff members and offer teaching demonstrations. Involve teachers, parents, and students in writing and sharing together.

Phone Calls

Contact parents by phone when a student is doing something well. Don't let the large number of students you teach prevent you from making this effort. Simply keep the call brief and be precise and positive about a student's achievement, a good grade, an act of kindness, or some special quality. Once you've established positive communication, it's much easier to contact parents later, if necessary. Unfortunately, most parents report they hear from a teacher or the school only when there is a problem.

Notes, Cards, Letters, Presentations, and Newsletters

Keep the lines of communication open. If you cannot reach a parent by phone, send a note or card. Letters are helpful in keeping parents up-to-date about long-term assignments or student achievement. Design several assignments with parents in mind. (A writing assignment that involves interviewing a family member works well.) With the student's permission, mail a copy of a best, final draft along with a cover letter explaining the assignment to his or her parent.

Invite parents and community members to class on days when students are sharing their work or presenting culminating response projects. Inform the local newspaper, as well, and suggest it run a feature highlighting a particular classroom activity. Celebrate students' successes and include parents in these celebrations.

Duplicate and mail a monthly or quarterly classroom newsletter to parents. Include samples of students' work and explanations of assignments and class activities. Involve students in its production. Submit students' work to the district newsletter as well.

Problem Solving

It's difficult for parents to hear their child isn't doing well in school. No one likes to hear bad news, and parents frequently feel they have little power to make a situation better. Early in the school year, when a student begins having either academic or behavioral problems, document the problem. Keep a record of your observations in precise detail and include notes on your responses. Don't wait too long to contact parents. A parent who finds out about a student-teacher disagreement from the student without any information from the teacher is likely to become angry and may be slow to forget. Before making a phone call, outline exactly what it is you have observed and the steps you have taken to solve the problem. Be tactful and professional. Offer solutions. Ask for parental input. It's important that parents recognize you have the desire and the ability to work with them to help their son or daughter. Be sure to follow up your initial call with at least one additional progress report.

Reporting Student Progress

Rather than mailing deficiency notices to the parents of students who are failing, send a computerized periodic progress report with a brief personal note to every parent. If you do not have access to a computer grading program, develop a simple personal form similar to the following:

Student Progress Report

Name _____ Date _____

Course_____ Teacher _____

Number of Absences _____

	Excellent	Average	Poor
1. Attitude	____	____	____
2. Initiative	____	____	____
3. Ability to get along with others	____	____	____
4. Dependability	____	____	____
5. Quality of work	____	____	____

Grade _____

Comments/suggestions:

If you take the time to confer with students about their grades before mailing forms such as this, you can avoid misunderstandings. If you and the student disagree about a grade, check your calculations and either change the grade or explain why the grade is what it is. Then ask the students to tell their parents what their grade is going to be and why.

Parent-Teacher Conferences

A regularly scheduled parent-teacher conference isn't a good time to surprise parents with negative information about their child's performance. You'll want to deal with problems as soon as they occur or alert a parent before the scheduled conference date. Although scheduled conferences days limit the time you can spend with any one parent, they can be productive if they are well planned. Because you are likely to involve your students in self-evaluation throughout the year, it's especially important that you do this before a formal conference. The student self-evaluation form 2.4, "Describe Your Work in this Class," included in Chapter 2, is especially useful. (Many teachers encourage students to attend the conferences, as well.) Your goal is for parents to leave these conferences with a clear picture of how well their sons and daughters are doing. Keep the conference informal and positive. The following format is helpful in conducting a successful conference:

Guidelines for a parent-teacher conference.

1. Open with a positive comment concerning the student and his or her contribution to the class.
2. Show samples of the student's classwork as well as his or her self-evaluation. A student-assembled portfolio is ideal for this.
3. Point out the student's academic strengths.
4. Discuss the student's academic weaknesses.
5. Ask about the parents' expectations for the student.
6. Set goals for the next grading period.
7. Suggest help that can be given at home to overcome weaknesses.
8. Ask for additional parental questions and input.
9. End the meeting on a positive, upbeat note.

All of us want a good education for our students. Show parents they are important in achieving this goal, and encourage and enable them to participate. Most will respond positively in any way they can.

WORKING WITH TEACHERS AND ADMINISTRATORS

Cooperation is a key part of every profession. Business people virtually never work alone; health-care teams in hospitals practice in consultation with one another. Likewise, the ideal school district consists of many people working as a team. English teachers have an especially strong motive for cooperating with their fellow teachers. Because English overlaps all other fields, working with other teachers is vital. Naturally, we hope that every instructor in the school will reinforce the attitude that good English is important.

Teachers

An English department is a group of people who are united in common concerns—their teaching area and the education of their students. A well-organized, smoothly functioning department accomplishes a great deal and improves the professional life of all its teachers. As an individual teacher, you can help your department function effectively. Be positive. Attend department meetings. Stay involved. Share responsibility. An ideal department has good organization, strong leadership, well-thought-out philosophy and goals, and time for its members to plan and evaluate curricula and share and exchange successful teaching strategies. Unfortunately, in far too many schools the ideal department does not exist. Many departments meet so infrequently and are so powerless that they are simply a collection of people who teach in the same discipline and who jealously guard their ideas and teaching materials for fear that someone else will use them.

There are some things, however, every teacher can do to work cooperatively with others:

1. Seek out colleagues with similar philosophies and goals. Help and encourage one another. Plan together and set some ground rules for the use of shared ideas. Make it a policy to return borrowed materials promptly and in good condition.

2. Along with teachers in the same or compatible disciplines, write proposals for special projects or pilot programs. (See Chapter 9 for a further discussion of grant writing.)

3. Keep administrators and counselors informed about what is happening with these projects and in your classrooms.

4. Ask for advice from teachers you admire and respect, and in turn support others in positive ways.

5. Make an effort to balance negative discussions with humor and a positive outlook.

6. If you are a more experienced teacher, encourage and help new teachers.

7. If you are a new teacher, find other beginning teachers and share experiences and encourage one another.

8. Become a part of the school's formal mentor program if one exists.

School relationships can be fragile. If we've worked together for a time, we've gotten to know one another's personal lives. Some of us will repeat the same stories over and over. We'll each have our ups and downs: sickness, emotional crises, other difficulties. We'll occasionally get on one another's nerves. Despite this, we need friends and a support system for commiseration as well as celebration. We need to nurture these friendships, especially when we consider the many hours and days we spend together. Who else really understands what it's like to interact with 150 teenagers day after day?

Substitute Teachers

For those times when it is possible to predict in advance when a substitute teacher will be needed, you'll want to provide directions and materials tailored to your teaching unit and objectives. Ideally, you will also confer with the substitute teacher beforehand. Substitutes generally like to talk to the teacher prior to working in the classroom. The following is a helpful checklist as you write lesson plans for a substitute teacher:

_____ 1. Seating chart or some means of identifying each student

_____ 2. Directions and materials for taking attendance

_____ 3. A statement of goals and objectives for the day's lesson

_____ 4. All necessary teaching materials and handouts and an explanation of where they are located

_____ 5. A step-by-step set of directions for presenting the lesson (Don't anticipate or expect that most substitute teachers will have the same knowledge of English or your school's policies as you do. The more you write, the better. Plans that say, "Do independent study" or "Study for the test" are too vague to be helpful.)

_____ 6. A clear statement of what students are expected to do or produce

_____ 7. An explanation of how the substitute teacher might help and work with individual students

_____ 8. An explanation of what students are to do with their completed work (For example, is the work to be exchanged with other students and corrected and collected, kept in the student's folder until a following day, handed in and graded by the substitute, or handed in for the classroom teacher to evaluate and grade? Be sure an answer key is provided if the substitute teacher is to do the grading.)

_____ 9. An explanation of what students are to do if they complete their work before the end of the class period

_____10. An assignment for the following day

_____11. Information about students with special needs, students who have the potential to cause problems, or students who otherwise require special handling

_____12. The name and location of a nearby teacher to turn to or talk to if problems arise

_____13. An explanation of extra duties if these are a part of your own assignment on a particular day (hall duty or detention, for example)

_____14. A notation of any school activity (such as an assembly) which might disrupt the normal schedule

It's not always possible, of course, to predict when you will need a substitute teacher. For the times when it is necessary for a substitute teacher to be called on short notice, keep a clearly marked substitute teachers resource file available in a conspicuous location. In addition to items 1, 2, 11, and 12 from the list above, include one or two sets of manageable classroom activities or lesson plans for emergencies. (Many of the suggested activities discussed in the first chapters of this book can be adapted as a substitute teacher's emergency lesson plan.) An additional source you might also add to this resource file is *Substitute Teachers' Lesson Plans,* published in 1989 by NCTE. This is an excellent collection of single-class-period activities designed for the nonspecialist English substitute.

Substitute teachers are one of the most powerful public relations tools a teacher has. Although confidentiality is expected, it is only natural that substitutes will make judgments about the school system and your effectiveness as a teacher based upon their experiences in your classroom. A substitute teacher who finds a poor lesson plan or none at all, who cannot find the necessary materials, or who is not given enough information about classroom routines cannot help but feel negative about your classroom or the school. By creating the best environment possible for the substitute teacher, you will not only enhance your image as a teacher, but you will also ensure that educationally sound and manageable activities continue to happen in your classroom when you are away.

Administrators

Observe any faculty lounge and most of the criticism you'll hear there is directed at the administration. "They just don't understand us," we complain. Aren't all those assemblies, announcements on the intercom, and classroom interruptions an administrator's plot to destroy our effectiveness? Administrators are a perfect target for our frustration or anger. We hate it if they appear to "hide" in their offices and never really know what's going on in the school. We hate it if they appear indifferent to our problems and lack immediate solutions. We hate it if an administrator observes and evaluates our teaching and classrooms but knows little about our subject area. We hate it if administrators don't write well, if messages from the office are filled with sentence fragments, run-on sentences, or jargon. Most of us have spent a great deal of time complaining about inefficiency and bureaucracy. Some of us thrive on it.

The criticisms leveled against principals are endless. These are not true of every administrator, of course, and to be really fair, we should look at the school day from their point of view. Most are intelligent, fair, and professional. Their first interest may be improving instruction, but the nature of their work is to spend long hours handling paperwork, taking care of attendance and discipline problems, and talking with irate parents. They're caught between the district office and the teachers. Many don't have a strong support system of their own or the immediate positive feedback that most classroom teachers can expect.

There are a number of things you can do to make working with principals and other administrators more productive:

1. Be the best teacher you can be. That's the first priority. Good administrators will recognize and have confidence in your expertise, and they will support you.

2. Be reliable and professional. Show up for assemblies. Arrive and leave school on time. Volunteer for your share of committees. Carry your weight.

3. Avoid constant complaining. Know what changes are realistic and then work toward a positive solution. When you have a legitimate problem, one that an administrator can solve, seek him or her out—when you are calm, reasonable, positive, and optimistic.

4. Differentiate between a passing problem and a long-term problem. Don't overuse a principal. Work to solve classroom problems yourself before asking for assistance with one that won't go away. You might, for example, discuss a discipline problem with a colleague or counselor before involving a principal. Keep your priorities in mind, and don't use up your goodwill on things that aren't essential.

5. Express your satisfaction and thanks for something done well.

Administrative observation.

In many schools, a formal plan for an administrator's observation of a teacher's performance is designed cooperatively by the school district's teachers and administrators and is agreed upon contractually. If this is the case in your school, be sure you understand the procedure for such an observation. On the other hand, if administrative observation and evaluation of your work in the classroom consists primarily of a principal "dropping in" from time to time, there are some things you can do to make an observation more productive and helpful. You can, for example, ask that an administrator evaluate your work in a more formal way. Request a formal observation and set a date. Design a lesson plan that will be helpful to anyone observing your work, and submit the plan to the observer before the date of the observation. Ideally, a lesson plan for a formal observation will include the following information:

1. An explanation of your objectives: What will the students know or be able to do following this lesson?

2. An explanation of where you are in the course or unit: Is this an introductory, middle, or culminating activity?

3. A description of the teaching methods you will use: Will you demonstrate, lecture, ask the students to work cooperatively in groups, or provide a practice exercise?

4. An explanation of the learning activities in which the students will be involved: Will students work independently, with partners, or in groups? What will they do?

5. An explanation of your evaluation process: How will you assess your students? How will you know they have learned?

6. A description of any special circumstances of which the observer should be aware: unusual behaviors or students leaving class during the period, for example.

A detailed lesson plan helps the observer respond fairly and helpfully, particularly if English is not his or her discipline. Following such an observation, ask to meet formally with the observer, and invite comments and suggestions and set personal goals.

Support Personnel

Some of the most important people in any school are those who perhaps receive the least recognition: secretaries, cooks, janitors, bus drivers, teacher's aides, and technicians. They contribute significantly to the effectiveness of a well-run school. Treat these people with courtesy and respect. Don't expect or demand unnecessary favors. Do learn and follow the prescribed procedures when requesting services. Be pleasant and grateful for the support and help when it is given.

WORKING WITH COMMUNITY RESOURCES

Many school districts have a formal community resource volunteer program. These are excellent programs that offer community members' knowledge, expertise, and talents to students in the classroom and enable a teacher to draw on the wealth of resources within the community. Most formal programs offer a catalog that lists widely varied topics and saves a teacher time in searching for volunteers. Most also have a formal request form to be filled out by the teacher, who sends it to the community resource office. The office makes the original contact with the volunteer, arranges the time and date, and confirms this information with the teacher. These programs also ask the teacher to complete a formal evaluation of a presentation to help plan better programs as well as give volunteers assistance in improving their presentations.

If your district has no formal resource program, begin making your own list or a departmental list of community resource people. As your students explore a specific theme in literature, for example, invite community people with expertise in this area to speak about their own experiences or knowledge of the topic. Invite local poets and writers, college and university staff members, and business leaders into your classroom. Contact human resource departments of large companies or go directly to the owners of small businesses. You might, for example, create an entire unit in which you ask several volunteers to speak about the importance of writing in their lives. Include cross-discipline resources, as well. Invite artists, art historians, musicians, actors, and performing groups into your classroom.

If you are making arrangements on your own, you'll need to be sure the guest has the following information:

1. Financial remuneration, if any: This must be cleared with the administration in advance. (See Chapter 9 for a discussion of grant applications.)

2. Topic and suggested format: Are you requesting a lecture, a discussion, or a performance?

3. The age and grade level of the students.

4. A brief description of your curriculum and its relation to the topic.

5. A schedule: Are you expecting the guest to meet with one class, several, or the entire student body? Will the presentation be given once or several times? Indicate the exact times and length of each presentation.

6. A map of the school indicating where parking is available and clearly showing the site of the presentations. Provide a guest parking permit, if one is required.

7. Details of lodging, meals, and transportation, if applicable.

Resource people offer endless possibilities for curriculum enrichment. It is well worth your time to add this dimension to your curriculum.

Avoiding Burnout: Becoming a More Effective Teacher

- *Staying Healthy and Fit*
- *Becoming a More Effective Teacher*

CHAPTER IX

Avoiding Burnout: Becoming a More Effective Teacher

Sue:	*This has been a great day, but it's been a tough year.*
	I can think of only two good days all year.
Mary Lou:	*What were they?*
Sue:	*Today and tomorrow.*

Stress is a part of all our lives. Some is positive and necessary. We may be excited and tense watching a baseball game or acting in a community theater production, for example. Good stress peps us up and produces healthy relaxation. In contrast, stress involving persistent anger, frustration, or worry can threaten our health and lead to professional burnout. Individuals in the helping professions are especially prone to this condition since we give of ourselves and tend to receive too little positive response in return. Ironically those teachers who are most frequently affected by varying degrees of burnout are often the most productive, dedicated, and committed professionals.

STAYING HEALTHY AND FIT

Low-level burnout causes us to feel less enthusiastic, less energetic, less fulfilled. After a short time, however, these feelings usually go away. Unchecked, they can intensify. We may experience shortness of temper, impatience, lapsed concentration, and sleepless nights. In time we may lose our ability to cope with minor daily problems, suffer chronic fatigue, and become more and more detached and cynical. Sadly, some of the best teachers leave the profession because of unchecked, destructive burnout.

As teachers, our professional lives are intense and hectic. To be effective each of us must develop a personal system for resisting, deflecting, or reducing the effects of stress and burnout in a demanding profession. Every one of us, new teachers as well as more experienced teachers, must consciously guard against burnout. The following suggestions will help you stay healthy and productive:

Vary your routine.

We often work in isolated settings, and our lives seem to be ruled by bells or buzzers signaling each class period. There may be little you can do about the school's rigid six- or seven-period day, and it is wasted energy to worry about things you can't control. However, you do control what happens in your classroom each period. You set the tone

234

and design the schedule. Personalize your environment . Don't be afraid to have fun. Vary your routine, be yourself, keep a sense of humor, and trust your instincts. Occasionally set aside a lesson you have planned, and do something unexpected— games, puzzles, discussion, or a film, for example. Rearrange the furniture and desks from time to time.

Experiment once in a while. Try a new approach or technique or new materials. Don't be afraid to fail. A lesson doesn't have to be perfect the first time you do it. Avoid using the same lesson plans, the same unit plans, the same semester and year-long schedule over and over. Few are so perfect that they deserve endless repetition.

Vary your lunch time routine. Instead of eating with the same people day after day, seek out other colleagues and locations. Talk with people who stimulate you intellectually. Occasionally, lock your classroom door and eat alone, read, or listen to public radio. On another day, go for a walk. Although thirty minutes is obviously not long enough for a civilized meal, eat at a nearby fast-food restaurant once in a while or plan ahead with colleagues and have food delivered to the teachers' lounge.

Interact with colleagues and students between classes. If you've lapsed into a pattern of complaining, make an effort to talk to people in a more positive way. Remember to give genuine praise when you see the successes and accomplishments of others. Support your colleagues' projects and special interests, and they will support yours.

Setting priorities and manage your classroom efficiently.

Most of us feel overwhelmed by all that we believe must be accomplished in limited time. You'll feel confident and in control if you manage your time efficiently. For example:

- Prioritize your objectives and set realistic goals.
- Simplify and focus your curriculum.
- Eliminate tasks and assignments that have become obsolete.
- Revise assignments that are time-consumers rather than time-savers. If the end product isn't worth the effort involved, eliminate the task entirely or rework it so that it's manageable and valid.
- Set reasonable long- and short-term deadlines.
- Organize and manage your classroom so that students take responsibility for routine clerical tasks. Give students immediate feedback by letting them correct some of their own work.
- Expect your students to write frequently, but don't feel you must read and correct everything they do. If you grade individual papers, ask students to select one of several writings for evaluation, and even then, concentrate on and respond to only one or two elements in the writing. The long hours we have traditionally spent red-marking student papers have seldom translated into proportionate learning on the part of our students.
- Work efficiently during the school day, and make it a policy to take as little school work home as possible. When you do have papers to correct, avoid spending too much time chatting with co-workers. Work during your prep period and lunch period. Occasionally, plan days for students to read or work quietly as you evaluate and grade material at your desk.
- Make daily and weekly "to do" lists. Crossing items off when they' re completed will help you realize what you've accomplished.

Pamper yourself.

Too often we teachers become so obsessed with our self-imposed deadlines and high expectations that we neglect ourselves. To be effective you must have a healthy diet, plenty of sleep, and exercise. It's never easy to force yourself into physical activity after arriving home exhausted and spent. Nevertheless, those teachers who do exercise daily discover renewed energy. Practice relaxation exercises, walk, take part in aerobic exercise, or join a health club. Resist the temptation to devote excessive hours entirely to school work.

Keep a folder of your successes: thank-you letters from students and parents, notes from principals commending your performance, copies of student work that has special meaning. Don't lose sight of the good things you've accomplished. Writing in your own journal will help you keep your perspective and clarify problems, which often shrink when they are expressed in writing.

Get involved in outside activities.

Keep a balance between your work and your life outside the job. Separate teaching from your private life as much as possible. When you're away from school, don't worry about ungraded papers and unfinished lessons or talk about your classroom endlessly. Treat yourself to the things you enjoy—a good meal, a trip, some time alone. Develop interests that are different from education, and use the summer break and weekends to change your daily routine and pursue these interests. Volunteer for projects that you can realistically handle and enjoy. Develop friendships away from school that involve people who are not teachers. When you are with colleagues, avoid constant shoptalk.

Consider other options.

If you feel locked into a less-than-ideal position, investigating other possibilities will both help you realize your worth and clarify other opportunities:

- Participate in a faculty exchange.
- Arrange for a change of responsibility or teaching assignment within your district.
- Consider teaching abroad. The Fulbright Exchange Program arranges overseas teaching opportunities. Contact the United States Information Agency, 301 Fourth Street SW, Washington, D.C. 20547, or your personnel office for additional information.
- Take a sabbatical for further study.
- Use a leave of absence to explore other options.
- Keep an up-to-date résumé so that you're prepared when other positions or options become available.

Be sure to guard your job security, however. Don't, for example, resign in frustration—you may discover you can't find anything else you like as well.

BECOMING A MORE EFFECTIVE TEACHER

As teachers we are members of one of the great professions. Each of us has the responsibility to be as effective as we can be. Each of us needs to grow professionally.

Self-evaluation

We spend much of our time judging and evaluating the performance of others: our students, peers, parents, and administrators. Even so, it's never quite easy to look at ourselves critically. Yet we must, if we want to be effective in our classrooms. The following suggestions are helpful ways for you to evaluate your own work in the classroom as you seek to improve your professional skills:

1. Once a semester make an audio- or videotape of one of your classroom sessions. Review the tape. Did the planned activities actually occur? Did they have the intended outcomes? What do you do well? What might you improve? Set personal goals each semester.

2. Team with a supportive colleague and observe one another's classrooms. Sit down together and honestly analyze each other's work. Note strengths as well as areas needing improvement. Talk about teaching strategies and better ways to teach.

3. Establish a class suggestion box and encourage students' suggestions.

4. Invite student evaluation of assignments and units rather than asking for a single evaluation at the end of the semester or year. For example:

- What do you like about this activity?
- What did you find most effective in the way we approached this activity?
- What do you feel is the most important thing you learned as you completed this activity?
- What should I change or do differently if I use this activity another year?

5. Elicit group discussion and evaluation midway in a course. For example:

- What about this class has been best at helping you learn the material?
- What can we do to improve this class?
- Is there anything you do not understand? What would you like to have reviewed or clarified?

6. Plan for an end-of-the-year evaluation. You might, for example, ask students to write letters to next year's students describing your class, explaining what to expect in terms of assigned work and classroom environment and offering advice on how to succeed. Form 9.1, "Course Evaluation," provides a helpful format. In using a form such as this, however, keep your students' responses in perspective. Don't be destroyed or even dismayed if one out of a hundred students hates his or her desk, dislikes you, and can't stand change. No teacher can succeed with every student, although we all try.

7. Write your own end-of-the-year evaluation.

8. If you are a less experienced teacher seek out a mentor. If you are a more experienced teacher work with a less experienced teacher. Mentorships, either formal or informal, can include any of the following elements:

- Regularly scheduled, confidential meetings
- Discussions concerning lesson plans, questions, problems, attendance, grade reporting, classroom management, or motivation strategies (Discussions on a variety of topics might also occur in a joint dialogue journal.)
- Observations of each other's classrooms
- Sharing of classroom materials, professional books, and magazines

9.1   Course Evaluation

Name of Course _____   Date _____

Please react to the following statements by circling the number which corresponds to how you feel about this class.

		I agree				I disagree
1. Directions are clearly given.		5	4	3	2	1
2. Grading is done fairly.		5	4	3	2	1
3. There is adequate time to complete assignments.		5	4	3	2	1
4. New ideas are accepted.		5	4	3	2	1
5. I have a chance to express my ideas.		5	4	3	2	1
6. The teacher gives extra help when needed.		5	4	3	2	1
7. The teacher knows the subject.		5	4	3	2	1
8. The subject is interesting.		5	4	3	2	1
9. The subject is not my favorite, but the teacher makes it interesting.		5	4	3	2	1
10. I have learned a lot in this class.		5	4	3	2	1

11. Please complete the following sentence: My favorite assignment was _____

_____

_____

_____

_____

12. Please complete the following sentence: If I taught the class, I would_____

_____

_____

_____

_____

© 1994 by The Center for Applied Research in Education

Staying Current

The most effective teachers never stop being curious, never stop reading, and never stop learning. Be informed about educational issues. Know what is happening at the local, state, and national levels. Understand your contract. Encourage your local teachers' organization to take progressive stands on issues.

Fortunately we have many options for professional growth. The National Council of Teachers of English and its state affiliates are organizations that every English teacher should join. The NCTE publishes a half dozen magazines, including the *English Journal,* geared specifically to keep secondary teachers abreast of current trends and research. It also publishes pamphlets and books on curricular and other matters and makes available to its members large numbers of teaching aids. *Notes Plus* offers many practical, hands-on activities a teacher can use immediately.

In addition to its publications, the NCTE holds national conventions that offer significant opportunities for continuing education, both in formal sessions and in informal discussions with other teachers from throughout the country. These conventions allow us to hear and respond to the leaders of our profession and provide a much needed professional stimulus to all teachers of English.

As a professional, consider acquiring an advanced degree. Enroll in college and university courses in your own and/or complementary disciplines.

You'll also want to begin or add to your professional library. As you do so, consider the following publications:

Periodicals

Contemporary Education	School of Education Indiana State University Terre Haute, IN 47809
Educational Leadership	Association for Supervision and Curriculum Development 1250 North Pitt Street Alexandria, VA 22314
Education Digest	Prakken Publications, Inc. 416 Longshore Drive Ann Arbor, MI 48107
English Journal	National Council of Teachers of English Urbana, IL 61801
Kappan	Phi Delta Kappa Eighth and Union P.O. Box 789 Bloomington, IN 47402
The New York Times Book Review	229 West 43rd Street New York, NY.10036
Notes Plus	National Council of Teachers of English Urbana, IL 61801

The Speech Communication Teacher	Speech Communication Association 5105 Backlick Road, Bldg. E. Annandale, VA 22003
Teacher Magazine	Editorial Projects in Education Suite 250, 4301 Connecticut Avenue N.W. Washington, DC 20008

Books

Atwell, Nancy. *In the Middle: Writing, Reading, and Learning with Adolescents.* Heinemann, 1987.

Glasser, William. *Control Theory in the Classroom.* Harper, 1986.

Macrorie, Ken. *Searching Writing.* Boynton/Cook, 1984.

Purves, Alan C. Theresa Rogers, and Anna O. Soter. *How Porcupines Make Love II: Teaching a Response Centered Literature Curriculum.* Longman, 1990.

Rubin, Louis J. *Artistry in Teaching.* Random, 1985.

Applying for Grants, Workshops, and Seminars

Improve your professional skills by attending local inservices and workshops. Most districts have staff development funds earmarked for individual and school- or districtwide projects and encourage teachers to develop projects either cooperatively or individually. Be sure you understand how these funds are allocated in your district. Why not, for example, apply for funds to pay for a substitute for your classroom for a day while you observe teachers in your own or another school?

Apply for summer institutes and seminars. The Fulbright Seminars Abroad program is open to secondary school teachers. Application forms are available from:

Fulbright Seminars Abroad Program
Center for International Education
U.S. Department for Education
400 Maryland Avenue SW
Washington, DC 20202
(202) 245-2794

The National Endowment for the Humanities offers both summer seminars and Masterwork Study Grants for secondary teachers. The Masterwork grant usually supports activities during the academic year but can involve summer study as well. For general information, guidelines, and application forms contact:

The National Endowment for the Humanities
Division of Education Programs, Room 302
1100 Pennsylvania Avenue, NW
Washington, DC 20506

In addition, a wide variety of grants are available from a variety of other sources. These grants are usually appropriated to institutions or in some cases to individuals for specific purposes. In making an application, you'll want to work with your district's designated grantwriter. If your district has no such person, you'll need to become knowledgeable about the grantwriting process.

Identify your need and goal.

Student scores in your school may be low in a particular area. A needs assessment may have indicated a specific problem. Your district or department may have determined a series of educational priorities. Any of these areas can become the focus of a grant application.

Know the type of grants available.

There are a variety of grants available: research grants, development grants, literacy grants, demonstrations grants, and replication grants. You'll need to determine which type of grant will best address your particular situation. For example, a replication grant will enable you to duplicate an existing successful program in another school. A research grant is intended to help you develop a program specifically designed for your individual situation.

Select the appropriate funding source.

Many publications offer information about available funds.

- *Education Grants Alert* is a weekly report on funding opportunities for K-12 programs.
- *Foundations & Corporate Grants Alert* and *Federal Grants and Contracts Weekly* detail areas of grant availability, application requirements, and dates and amounts awarded. For more information about these publications, call 1-703-683-4100.
- *The Foundation Directory* and *Foundations Grants Index Bimonthly* published by The Foundation Center (1-800-424-9836) describe thousands of corporate, community, and independent foundations that award grants.
- The *Federal Register,* a daily government publication, provides up-to-date reporting of federal grants.

With so many grants available, it's important that you determine the most appropriate funding source for your project. By carefully analyzing each grant listing, you will be able to determine which program areas this source is funding as well as information pertaining to proposal requirements, application dates, eligibility, and dollar amounts awarded.

Submit a clearly and concisely written proposal.

The format and degree of comprehensiveness required in a written proposal vary from source to source, and you will need to read the particular guidelines. Most proposals, however, usually include the following components:

- cover letter
- title page
- narrative description
- needs
- objectives
- activities

- personnel
- evaluation procedures
- budget

Many grant writers suggest that one of the best ways to include all the components and specific information necessary for a good proposal is to focus on *who, what, where, when* and *how* and relate each to the overall purpose and goal of the project. It's also important that you present a realistic and reasonable scenario regarding program implementation and cost. Mail your proposal via registered mail, return-receipt requested, before the deadline.

References

Chapter I.

[1]Margaret Wilson Kuehn. *Notes Plus.* Dec., 1992. NCTE: Urbana, Illinois: pp. 6–7.

Chapter II.

[1]William Wayson, ed. *Handbook for Developing Schools with Good Discipline.* Bloomington, Indiana: Phi Delta Kappa Commission on Discipline, 1981, p. 29.

[2]Corwin Kronenberg. *A Positive Approach to Discipline.* (unpublished manuscript) Bloomington, Minnesota, 1992.

[3]William Glasser. *Control Theory in the Classroom.* Harper, l986, pp. 1–30.

[4]*New Teacher's Handbook.* New York: Impact II, 1988, p. 25.

[5]Leon Paulsen, Pearl R. Paulsen, and Carol A. Mayer. "What Makes a Portfolio a Portfolio?" pre-publication draft, September, 1990.

[6]Elaine Greenspan, *Beyond Survival.* Portland, Maine: J. Weston Walch, 1987, pp. 22–26.

Chapter III.

[1]Stephen N. Judy and Susan J. Judy. *The English Teacher's Handbook.* Boston: Scott, Foresman and Company, l983, pp. 26–27.

[2]Richard D. Lavoie. *Understand Learning Disabilities: How Difficult Can This Be?* (video) Greenwich, Connecticut: Eagle Hill School Outreach, 1989.

[3]*Ibid.*

[4]Lynne Chalmers. *Modifying Curriculum for the Special Needs Student in the Regular Classroom.* Moorhead, Minnesota: Practical Press, 1992, pp. 1–5.

Chapter IV.

[1]David W. Johnson, Roger T. Johnson, and Edythe Johnson Holubec, eds. *Cooperation in the Classroom.* Edina, Minnesota: Interaction Book Co., 1991. p. 2:8. (Another helpful book by the same editors is *Structuring Cooperative Learning: Lesson Plans for Teachers,* Edina, Minnesota: Interaction Book Co., 1987. This source offers complete lesson plans for teachers in a wide variety of academic areas and grade levels.)

[2]*Ibid.*

[3]George Hillock quoted by Martin Nystrand, Adam Gamoran, and Mary Jo Heck in "Using Small Groups for Response to and Thinking about Literature," *English Journal,* Vol. 82, Jan. l993, p. 14.

[4]"The Real World?" *Writing* (Teacher's Edition), Vol. 15, No. 4, December, l992, p. 6.

[5]Johnson, Johnson, and Holubec, eds., p. 1:22.

[6]Johnson, Johnson, and Holubec, eds., p. 2:13.

Chapter V.

[1]Mary Ellen Schoonmaker. "Children as Authors: Building an Early Foundation for Writing." *Education Week,* October 10, 1984, p. 10.

[2]*A Guide to Curriculum Planning in English Language Arts.* Madison, Wisconsin: Wisconsin Department of Public Instruction, l986, pp. 124–129.

[3]Harvey Daniels and Steven Zimmerman. *A Writing Project: Training Teachers of Composition from Kindergarten to College.* Portsmouth, New Hampshire: Heineman Books, l985, pp. 1–20.

[4]Gabriele Rico. *Writing the Natural Way.* Los Angeles: J.P. Tarcher, Inc., 1983, pp. 63–87, 90.

[5]Marty Brewster. "Rooming with Characters," *English Journal.* October, 1988, pp. 65–66.

[6]Stephen Dunning and William Stafford. *Getting the Knack.* Urbana, Illinois: NCTE, 1992.

[7]*The NWEA Direct Writing Assessment Prompt Collection.* Salem, Oregon: Northwest Evaluation Association, l989, pp. 30, 104.

[8]Jean Borax. "Brian's Totally Awesome Vacation Journal," *Starting from Scratch: A Writing Manual.* St. Paul, Minnesota: Dialogue Assessment Project of the St. Paul Public Schools, 1992.

[9]Norita Dittberner-Jax. "Responding to Writing: Special Concerns," *Starting from Scratch.* St. Paul, Minnesota: Dialogue Assessment Project of the St. Paul Public Schools, 1992, p. 51.

[10]John Caddy. "I-Referenced Responses to Writing" (unpublished manuscript.) St. Paul, Minnesota: COMPAS, 1989.

[11]Nancy Carlyon Milett. *Teaching the Writing Process.* Boston: Houghton Mifflin Company, 1986, p. 27.

[12]*A Guide to Surviving the Teaching of Writing.* Madison, Wisconsin: Wisconsin Department of Public Instruction, l985, pp. 27–33.

[13]Marlene Scardamalia and Carl Bereiter. "Research on Written Composition," *Handbook of Research on Teaching.* New York: Macmillan, l986, pp. 778–803.

[14]*Writing Across the Curriculum.* Memphis, Tennessee: Memphis City Schools, Division of Curriculum Development, 1988, p. 52.

[15]Jessica O. Ellis. "Cooperative Learning in English," *English Journal,* October, l990, p. 75.

[16]*A Guide to Surviving the Teaching of Writing,* p. 42.

[17]David England. "Teaching Writing Process and Determining Grades," *Quarterly of the National Writing Project and Center for the Study of Writing.* August, l986, pp. 18–21, 27.

[18]Edgar Thompson. "Self-Assessment and the Mastery of Writing," *Testing in the English Arts: Uses and Abuses.* Rochester, Michigan: Michigan Council of Teachers of English, 1985, pp. 55–60.

[19]Jean Jensen. "Career Research: Researching for Real," *English Journal,* September, l989, pp. 39–40.

[20]Beverly A. McColley. "Achieving Verisimilitude," *English Journal,* October, 1988, p. 72.

[21]Rosemarie Stocky. "Round Table," *English Journal,* October, 1988, p. 74.

[22]*Learning and Writing,* St. Paul, Minnesota: St. Paul Public Schools, l986, pp. 103–107.

[23]*Successful Strategies for Writing in Content Areas,* St. Paul, Minnesota: St. Paul Public Schools, n.d., pp. 27–29.

[24]Margo Kriel Galt. *Program Resource Manual: Activities and Lesson Plans for Using the Writing Process.* St. Paul, Minnesota: COMPAS, 1988, pp. 27–28.

[25]Laurie Lawlor. "Words from Laurie Lawlor," *Writing,* May, 1991, p. 26.

Chapter VI.

[1]Louise Rosenblatt. *Literature as Exploration.* New York: Noble and Noble, 1968, pp. 1–50.

[2]Nancy Atwell. *In the Middle: Writing, Reading, and Learning with Adolescents.* Portsmouth, New Jersey: Boynton/Cook, 1986, pp 25.

[3]*Ibid.,* pp. 19–22.

[4]Stephen N. and Susan J. Judy. *The English Teacher's Handbook: Ideas and Resources for Teaching English.* Glenview, Illinois: Scott, Foresman and Company, 1983, p. 111.

[5]Richard Beach, Marsha Besch, and Canda Haga. *Using Guided Assignments to Teach Literature.* St. Paul, Minnesota: Minnesota Department of Education, 1986, p. 6.

[6]Alan C. Purves, Theresa Rogers, and Anna O. Soter. *How Porcupines Make Love II: Teaching a Response-Centered Literature Curriculum.* New York: Longman, 1990, pp. 47–84.

[7]Jane Ann Zaharias. "Literature Anthologies in the U.S.: Impediments to Good Teaching Practice," *English Journal,* October, 1989, pp. 22–27.

[8]Diane P. Shugert. "How to Write a Rationale in Defense of a Book," *Dealing with Censorship.* James E. Davis, ed. Urbana, Illinois: NCTE, 1979, 187–191.

[9]"Stories to be Read Aloud," *English Journal,* February, l989, pp. 87–90.

[10]J.N. Hook and William H. Evans. *The Teaching of High School English.* New York: Macmillan Publishing Company, 1982, p. 154.

[11]Anne Haas Dyson, ed. *Collaboration through Writing and Reading.* Urbana, Illinois: NCTE, 1989, p. 192.

[12]Patricia Gunderlach. *Notes Plus,* January, l993, Urbana, Illinois: NCTE, pp. 1–2.

[13]Elfie Israel. "Showing Mastery through Performance," *English Journal,* March, 1993, pp. 69–70.

[14]Joanne Paprocki. "Poet-tees," *Notes Plus,* March, l993, Urbana, Illinois: NCTE, p. 7.

Chapter VII.

[1]*Model Learner Outcomes.* St. Paul, Minnesota: Minnesota Department of Education, 1988, pp. 19–24.

[2]For many excellent suggestions see *Classroom Activities in Listening and Speaking* published in l991 by the Wisconsin Department of Public Instruction. This source provides a listening and speaking sequenced curriculum with classroom activities for elementary, middle school, and secondary classrooms.

[3]Ron Padgett. "Creative Reading," *Teachers and Writers,* May–June, 1990, p. 7.

[4]*Classroom Activities in Listening and Speaking,* pp. 34–35.

[5]M. Kozacik. "Doodles and Directions," *Substitute Teachers' Lesson Plans.* Urbana, Illinois: NCTE, l989, pp. 5–6.

[6]David W. Johnson, Roger T. Johnson, and Edythe Johnson Holubec, eds. *Cooperation in the Classroom.* Edina, Minnesota: Interaction Book Company, 1991, p. 3:33.

[7]James Moffett and Betty Jane Wagner. *Student-Centered Language Arts and Reading, K–13.* Boston: Houghton Mifflin Company, p. 74.

[8]Judith Chapman. *Feminist Resources for Schools and Colleges.* New York City: The Feminist Press, 1986, pp. 1–20.

[9]*Ibid.*

[10]Johnson, Johnson, and Holubec, eds., p. 2:24.

[11]Candy Carter and Zora M. Rashkis, eds. *Ideas for Teaching English in the Junior High and Middle School.* Urbana, Illinois: NCTE, p. 214.

[12]*Classroom Activities in Listening and Speaking,* pp. 50, 56.

[13]Marcy Urban. "Video Biographies: Reading, Researching, and Recording," *English Journal,* December, 1989, pp. 58–59.

Chapter VIII.

[1]Peggy Gisler and Marge Eberts. "Dear Teacher," *Star Tribune,* Jan. 26, 1992, p. 4Ex.